THE BEVERLY HILLBILLIES

STEPHEN COX

FOREWORD BY
BUDDY EBSEN

OB
CONTEMPORARY
BOOKS
CHICAGO · NEW YORK

Library of Congress Cataloging-in-Publication Data

Cox, Stephen D., 1948–
   The Beverly Hillbillies.

   1. Beverly Hillbillies (Television program)   I. Title.
PN1992.77.B46C6   1988   791.45'72   88-25831
ISBN 0-8092-4504-3 (pbk.)

Copyright © 1988
All rights reserved Stephen Cox
Published by Contemporary Books, Inc.
180 North Michigan Avenue, Chicago, Illinois 60601
Manufactured in the United States of America
International Standard Book Number: 0-8092-4504-3

Published simultaneously in Canada by Beaverbooks, Ltd.
195 Allstate Parkway, Valleywood Business Park
Markham, Ontario L3R 4T8 Canada

To my loving parents, Gerald and Blanche Cox, who cared enough to give a fantastic home to one Canadian child and three Irish children. Also to *our* little Granny.

And to Paul and Irene, two dedicated individuals who put so much love into the series.

Contents

COURTESY OF GABI RONA

Jed, the cornerstone of the Clampett Clan.

FOREWORD

"Tell me, Mr. Ebsen, when you all started making this 'Beverly Hillbillies' series, had you any idea it was going to be the smashing success that it turned out to be?"

That is the question most frequently asked by people everywhere about "The Beverly Hillbillies." Obviously, everyone who worked on the show must have thought it had something.

It would have been fun if we had all written down our predictions and sealed them in a time capsule, but I don't think even the most optimistic would have slotted us for the number one spot right from the starting gun. That includes Paul Henning, the charming little giant who dreamed it all up, for his talent is only exceeded by his modesty and conservatism. It was a funny idea, a good gamble, and we were all determined to give it our best, then see what happened.

And this is how I acquired the most diverting and enjoyable family I have ever known outside of my own.

Best wishes
Buddy Ebsen

Buddy Ebsen

Recording star Roy Clark, in his acting debut, plays both cousin Roy Halsey and Halsey's mother, Myrtle.

PHOTO BY VIACOM

A WORD FROM ROY CLARK

In 1968, I portrayed "Cousin Roy" in three episodes of "The Beverly Hillbillies." And in doing so, there were a few "firsts" that impressed me.

By this time, I was getting recognized in the business and had performed on most all of the variety shows, but this role was my television acting debut.

Also, Donna Douglas was my first screen kiss—not a bad way to start.

Finally, what really impressed me and what I admired most about the show was it was the first to use real country music as the theme. It almost amazed me because most country and rural shows used orchestras. The authentic theme, supplied by my friends Flatt and Scruggs, was great.

And because this field was new to me and I was nervous, all of the cast made me feel right at home and they were great to work with. Right from the initial read-through, I felt a lot better about it. I wasn't sure I could pull off the job of playing my own mother as well.

Buddy Ebsen invited me into his dressing room, which was like a little house on the set. He was studying guitar, so we picked a little bit. He invited me to have lunch with him and went out of his way to make me feel comfortable. You can see why I had fun.

A book on "The Beverly Hillbillies" is a great idea. The audience is out there, and the show was a part of people's lives for so long that it shouldn't be forgotten. Thanks to this book, it won't.

In fact, to this day, because of the reruns, people will walk up to me and say, "I saw you on TV last night!" and I thank them for watching. "Yeah, I sure loved that plaid suit ya had on."

I know immediately what that's from—"The Beverly Hillbillies."

Roy Clark
March 1988

THANK YA KINDLY

The author wishes to thank the following folk fer lendin' a heapin' helpin' of their time and effort to make this an enjoyable book: Carol Anderson, Rob Austin, Gloria Buckles, George Carney, Roy Clark, Kingsley Colton, Brian Cury, Joe Depew, Peter Engler, George Faber, Jeff Forrester, Tom Forrester, Dale Freeman, George Getz, Mark Gilman, Phil Gordon, Shad and Molly Heller, Linda Kaye Henning, Bob Hope, John Horvath, Scott Hunker, Frank Inn, Jean Jensen, Nancy Kane, Sammy Keith, Cathy Keller, John Lofflin, Sandy Mailliard, Curt and Edythe Massey, Mark Noe (Park College Communication Arts Department), Don Richardson, Norm Robertson, Gabi Rona, Al Simon, Dave Strauss, Stylus staff, Ted Switzer, Frederick Tucker, Elena Watson, Marty and Mimi Williams, Michelle Yohe.

And these organizations: CBS, (Howard Frank/Personality Photos Inc., P.O. Box 50, Midwood Station, Brooklyn, N.Y. 11230), Kellogg's Company, Silver Dollar City, and Viacom International, Inc.

Most of all, a special tip o' the hat for the personal attention from: Gerald and Blanche Cox, Paul and Ruth Henning, and the cast: Max Baer, Donna Douglas, Buddy Ebsen, Nancy Kulp. And to my editor, Susan Buntrock, who loves "fun" books.

INTRODUCTION

There is not a show in television history that has equaled the achievements of "The Beverly Hillbillies." No other show has reached number one in such a short amount of time. No other show gave new meaning and instant recognition to words; the show popularized *hillbilly, vittles,* and *Granny.* And no other show can claim eight entries in the Nielsen Ratings list of top-rated individual episodes of all time—all in the top twenty.

It's doubtful that any other show has received such despicable press yet attained such fantastic ratings from the very beginning. The critics hated the Clampetts. The viewers loved Jed, Granny, Jethro, and Elly May. For nine years, the Hillbillies kept up their cornball antics while remaining in the top twenty. Truly, they deserve recognition—which the Emmys never gave.

Thus, the words *legend* and *genius* can be unquestionably applied to "The Beverly Hillbillies."

Paul Henning, the creator, writer, and producer, is clearly the "genius." The show's success and style make it "legendary."

For these reasons, I welcome you to enjoy a heapin' helpin' of this little history about a TV show that many people, young and old, love. For this, the twenty-fifth anniversary of a show that remained number one in the United States all of 1963—and sustained an unsurpassed rank—we celebrate.

Stephen Cox

1
HILLS THAT IS: SWIMMIN' POOLS, MOVIE STARS . . . HILLBILLIES?

It had never happened in the history of television and might never happen again. When the second episode of a peculiar little show about a mountain family was aired, more than thirty-six million viewers cast votes electing the Clampett clan as TV's first family.

Television critics from coast to coast were appalled that the medium could stoop to such corncob humor. "We're liable to be Beverly Hillbillied to death," said TV conscience David Susskind. "Please write your Congressman." But while the critics growled, the public howled. America loved the Beverly Hillbillies and their simple, down-home, corny gags. The public raised the Clampetts onto a pedestal so high that their popularity fattened the wallets of CBS almost instantaneously.

The Saturday Evening Post reported that "Hillbillies madness spread: juke boxes began blaring the show's banjo theme, army-and-navy stores reported a boom in plaid-shirt and blue jean sales, and network executives started ordering similar pasto-rales for future airing."

The decision was in: these Beverly bumpkins not only hit Californy, they hit America—hard!

This was not a mere rehash of the motion pictures' Ma and Pa Kettle, nor was it a takeoff of ABC's "The Real McCoys." For Paul Henning, the creator of "The Beverly Hillbillies"—and soon to be its writer and producer and the overall energy that fueled it to

PHOTO BY GABI RONA

These backwoods bumpkins are mistaken for gardeners when they arrive at their mansion in the hills of Beverly.

nine years on television—it was an idea that struck him while vacationing across the country with his wife, Ruth, and his mother-in-law. He explained:

After "The Bob Cummings Show" in '59, I took Ruth's mother on a long motor trip. I think we covered fourteen thousand miles.

We drove through the South and had just visited a historical Civil War site when I said, "Wouldn't it be interesting to think of the reaction of someone from that period, say the 1860s, to put them suddenly in the back seat of the car going along seventy miles an hour? They'd be astonished!"

That idea kind of stayed with me. I wondered how, without being too magic, such a thing could be accomplished. I subsequently read a little bit about someone trying to build a road through a remote section of the Ozark Mountains and how the residents would try to stop the building of the road. They didn't want to have access. Part of that, I'm sure, was that a lot of them made their living moonshining and they didn't want "fereners," as they called it, coming in the remote places.

Al Simon and the president at Filmways heard I liked Hillbilly humor and offered to buy the TV rights for Ma and Pa

Kettle, but I said no. "If I'm gonna do a hillbilly program, I'm gonna do my own and create it myself."

Henning penned the concept on paper and finally made the decision to do something about it. Only days later, he arranged a luncheon appointment at the Brown Derby Restaurant with Al Simon and Marty Ransohoff, the executives of Filmways Television.

"I told them the concept," Henning says of his original undertaking for the hit series. "These hillbillies strike oil and move to a sophisticated urban center, which I first imagined to be New York. But then I got to thinking of the cost of filming in New York and how it wouldn't work. Where else could they land? I thought of Beverly Hills, which is about as sophisticated as you can get on the West Coast."

Henning explained the story based on a few character sketches from his notebook, including an abundant list of show ideas that he had jotted down already. By the end of lunch, the group had made a handshake deal.

The series was sold.

PHOTO BY STEPHEN COX

Executive producer Al Simon boasts today about the success of his heroes from Beverly Hills—also his place of residence.

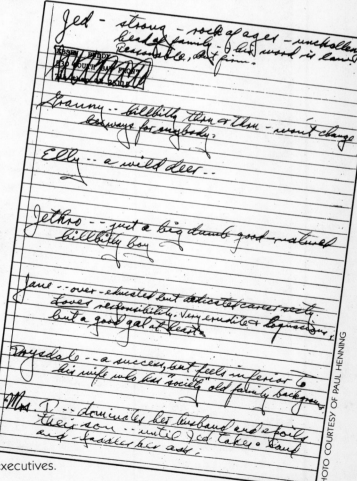

PHOTO COURTESY OF PAUL HENNING

The original Hillbilly character sketches Paul Henning used to pitch the show to Filmways executives.

Al Simon explains why he agreed to this corn-fed comedy so readily: "I thought automatically it was going to be the best thing that hit television in a long, long while. There was no question in my mind about it!"

Filmway's board chairman, Ransohoff, had negotiated a deal immediately, promising $100,000 of the company's money without a sponsor on the list yet. He was that sure of the show—and of this writer's talent.

CASTING

After the script for the pilot episode, "The Hillbillies of Beverly Hills," was inked and passed between executives. The casting search was on. Casting was tedious for some roles, while Henning had specific actors in mind for others.

PHOTO BY GABI RONA

At the wheel of a 1921 rattletrap, Baer chauffeurs Buddy Ebsen, Donna Douglas, Duke, and Irene Ryan.

"I always had Buddy Ebsen in mind," says Henning of the patriarchal Clampett role. "He's a big man, but he moves as gracefully as a dancer would. He's kind of an ideal frontiersman, hillbilly, used to getting around in the woods."

Henning approached Ebsen, who hadn't acted much since his regular television role as George Russell, Davy Crockett's sidekick. At first, Ebsen wasn't enthusiastic about playing another backwoods role. He told reporters later, "My agent had mentioned the hillbillies. I wanted to run the other way. I had played a lot of hillbillies, and I just didn't want to get trapped again in that kind of getup with long hair and whiskers."

He took the part after talking with Henning, but first the two had to agree on one aspect: "It sounded like everyone was going to be very funny—everybody except me," Ebsen says. "Which was fine, provided I was still the pivotal character. I told Paul that I had to have control of the $25 million. If I do, I'll be the responsible member of the family and not merely the guy who's the butt of all the jokes! So he said sure."

After being handed the role, Ebsen had to endure the screen tests of the candidates for the rest of the roles. He remained, in costume, at the studio for many hours while hopefuls filed in to say their lines with Buddy on film for the producers. A test on film was mandatory, explains Simon: "There were many times in the room we thought somebody was very good, and in the test they were not. We had to look at their on-camera presence. We had to see what the screen said."

Finding an actress for the part of Granny was the toughest mission. Henning and Simon frequented many hillbilly bands and hoedowns around the Los Angeles area searching for the perfect little woman they had imagined.

"Finally, we found someone and thought, 'Gee, this woman's great. This is gonna work out' " says Simon. "She sounded great when we talked to her. She said she'd have her nephew, with whom she stayed, help her with the reading. When she came in and faced those cameras, she froze. She couldn't read! She was illiterate, but she disguised it cleverly."

Henning remembers that when he approached actress Bea Benaderet with the script, she said, "Oh let me audition for Granny!" Henning pictured Granny as a wiry little woman, but he let the endowed Bea audition anyway.

"My actual statement was, 'Bea, with those tits?' " Henning says. "Bea was stacked, you know. But when we did the test, she had seen Irene [Ryan] ready to go and do her thing. She said, 'There's your Granny!' "

Paul peered over to the other side of the studio where Ryan, a short little lady weighing no more than a hundred pounds, was preparing to test. At the prodding of her agent, Kingsley Colton,

COURTESY OF VIACOM

The twosome of Earl Scruggs (left) and
Lester Flatt, who recorded the theme song "The Ballad
of Jed Clampett," guest star as themselves, friends of
the Clampetts. Granny prefers to make it a trio.

Ryan had visited Paul in his office earlier in the week asking for
a test.

Ryan tested with Buddy Ebsen, and Henning had to agree with
Benaderet: this *was* Granny. The role of Cousin Pearl was given
to Benaderet. In fact, Benaderet was so good as wacky cousin
Pearl, Henning knew this talented, versatile comedienne needed
a vehicle of her own to star in. Later he would cast her as Kate
Bradley in "Petticoat Junction," another Henning hit.

COURTESY OF VIACOM

The two faces of Irene Ryan.

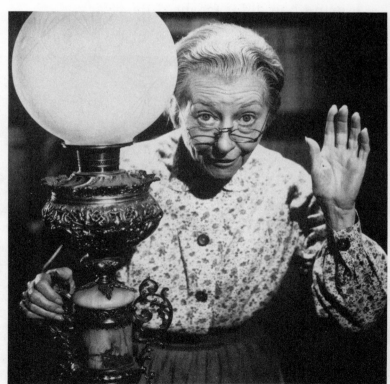

"Let's just say I'm older than Shirley Temple, but younger than Sophie Tucker."

COURTESY OF VIACOM

The casting of Donna Douglas as Elly May was nearly as easy.

"There was a girl who tested for Elly May, a redhead. She was a knockout. She was sensational," Henning remembers. "We gave her the part, but she took another job at Universal. I was so mad at her; I wouldn't have used her for free." Luck was with Donna Douglas; the part was now available.

As Donna explains:

> I was interviewed along with over a hundred girls, I think. When they told me I got the part, I thought my heart was gonna burst right open. I was looking for a role like this, a family show. To me, it was an opportunity to do quality work—something my parents and my son could be proud of.
>
> It was like God had trained me all my life to do that part. I already knew how to whistle and everything. And they never really had to give me any direction regarding Elly. I could tell you anything about Elly at any time, day or night. I knew Elly from day one.

In addition to the endless line of women to choose from for the part of Elly May, there was the lineup of men for the role of Jethro. Henning and Simon spent a full Saturday reviewing actors, among them Max Baer, Jr.

"When I tested, I laughed a lot, and they told me later the wide grin I had did it for me, " Baer says.

COURTESY OF VIACOM

One of the first publicity stills taken for the show. The characters were still wet behind the ears.

"THE HILLBILLIES OF BEVERLY HILLS"

In Henning's pilot, captured on 35-mm film for posterity, the Hillbillies, living in their mountain cabin, struck oil. The filming of the pilot, titled "The Hillbillies of Beverly Hills," went relatively smooth. It was shot in five days on location at the Beverly Hills reservoir in December 1961. Filmways built a little cabin on the location for Jed's mountain home right in the heart of Beverly Hills, California. It was as rustic and rural as any place in the Missouri Ozarks. Meanwhile, Filmways was preparing for the arrival of the Clampetts in the elite city of stars.

The studio built a huge set that resembled a Bel-Air mansion. The owner of the mansion-hideaway, Arnold Kirkeby, a Chicago hotel magnate, allowed the studio to film the exterior of his home for the show, but sets were built in the General Service studios for the production: an exterior of the house which led into the main lobby, a kitchen set, a parlor, a swimming pool, a Commerce Bank exterior, and an office for Drysdale. These sets and the lights remained stationary and relatively untouched so that the crew could have easy access to the set at any time.

COURTESY OF PAUL HENNING

The Kirkeby mansion in Bel-Air was used as the exterior for the first three years of the show. In the early 1980s, newspapers reported it sold for more than $25 million. Ronald and Nancy Reagan purchased a home nearby as their retirement retreat after his Presidency.

The Set: This was then one of the costliest sets con-
structed specificall; for a TV series. An estimated
$60,000 was spent building a pseudomansion on the
sound stage for the Hillbillies' Beverly Hills residence.
The foyer and the kitchen sets were where most of the
filming took place.

COURTESY OF PAUL HENNING

The Cee-ment Pond: This monstrosity of a set took a $20,000 chunk of the show's
budget. It was only twenty-seven inches deep, complete with filter and heating units.
Because of the vast air-conditioning system in the studio, the pool took nearly half of
the working day to heat. Behind the Doric columns was a painted, half-round
cyclorama of scenery that appeared to be Beverly Hills. Weeeellll, doggies, we was
slickered!

COURTESY OF PAUL HENNING

STRATEGIC SELLING OF THE SERIES

After the pilot was in the can, only the job of getting the series sold to the network and coming up with sponsors lay ahead. Originally the show was offered to ABC-TV, which passed it by. Henning, again, had a strategy. He and Al Simon decided on approaching their favorite advertising executive in New York, Sam Northcross, who also had worked on Henning's previous vehicle, "The Bob Cummings Show."

COURTESY OF VIACOM

Elly May, Jed, Granny, and Pearl don't know what to make of the chandelier in their swanky mansion. They think it's some sort of a wind chime for a drafty house.

Henning and Simon insisted on complete privacy regarding the pilot. They called Northcross, who immediately flew out to Hollywood. To avoid anyone viewing the pilot before Henning and Simon were ready, they gave Northcross an exclusive preview of the pilot late one night at the studio.

Northcross loved it and gave the account exclusively to the R. J. Reynolds Tobacco Company.

Simon recalls that CBS picked up the show but wanted to air it on "The GE Theater," which was then hosted by Ronald Reagan. But the agency who sponsored the show turned it down on the grounds that the pilot wasn't right for GE's audience.

"Now CBS had the pilot and they wondered what the hell to do with it. They still balked at the show's title, and preferred it to be called 'Head for the Hills' or 'The Hillbillies,' " says Simon. "But Henning held out, which proved wise when his choice was approved only weeks before airing. The fact that it was turned down by GE's sponsor made a lot of top CBS brass think that it wouldn't go."

Finally, CBS put the show opposite "The Perry Como Show," which was getting high ratings. However, Filmways felt CBS was doing very little to attract viewers, so it began to develop its own ideas.

Filmways bypassed the network and quickly cranked out a

PHOTO BY GABI RONA

The first publicity stills of Irene Ryan were not very flattering, since the makeup department attempted to transform her into the oldest woman alive. Her makeup was toned down after they realized the extra wrinkles weren't needed.

series of thirty-to-sixty-second trailers, or brief filmed previews, of the show.

"The words 'Beverly Hillbillies' were not going to get a lot of people to watch the show," says Al Simon. "And the most important medium you could have was television. We began thinking the best thing to do was to get the top thirteen stations with the largest audiences in the United States that would be carrying the show.

"Paul wrote very funny trailers and we had our publicity man contact every one of those stations and ask for their logos and told them we were doing personal trailers for that station. So before the show got on the air, everyone in those major markets knew about the Beverly Hillbillies."

Their strategy worked—even before airing, the show had a built-in audience. And the network affiliate took advantage of the personalized film and aired it continuously as free promotion.

The characters of Jed, Granny, Elly May, and Jethro were introduced in the trailers, and viewers got a sneak preview of the hillbilly humor that was about to capture them.

During the summer months of 1962, the seven publicity agents were also ordered to obey a strict edict put forth by Henning regarding his publicity strategy:

COURTESY OF KMOX-TV

MEET US IN ST. LOUIS: The gang says a special "Hillbilly hello" as they are introduced to the Gateway to the Midwest in this personalized trailer, shot for St. Louis's KMOX-TV.

Date: June 28, 1962

For the present, I would prefer that Buddy Ebsen, Irene Ryan, Donna Douglas, and Max Baer cease to exist as themselves. The dissemination and publication of personal biographies, idiosyncrasies, so-called squibs, blurbs, plants in columns, and photographic layouts of them at home are to be discouraged by every means at our disposal! NO STORY IS BETTER THAN THE WRONG STORY! . . . and a wrong story is one that damages the television image of our hillbilly characters.

Henning felt that the audience would have trouble believing in the hillbilly characters if it saw publicity layouts of Max Baer at a nightclub with some starlet or Buddy Ebsen on his yacht. His edict was strictly adhered to by publicity agents. Only in-costume, in-character publicity was allowed for the time being—until the show got running smoothly and the characters were imbedded in viewers' imaginations.

You can see these four are happy. They just received the ratings telling them they're number one in America.

COURTESY OF VIACOM

His ideas worked. The airing on that Wednesday night, September 26, 1962, captured 50 percent of the viewing audience. The second episode knocked "The Perry Como Show" off *TV Guide*'s map.

Two weeks later, says *The Saturday Evening Post*, "on location at the Bel-Air mansion, the cast members got word of their ascension to the top. Impulsively they formed a serpentine conga line and improvised a locomotive chant that went, 'We're number one! We're number one! We're number one!' "

Well, the Clampetts had arrived . . . in Beverly Hills, on television, and in America's heart.

As the theme song, "The Ballad of Jed Clampett" (lyrics and music by Paul Henning), says,

Come 'n listen to my story 'bout a man name Jed
Poor mountaineer, barely kept his fam'ly fed.
An' then one day, he was shootin' at some food,
An' up thru the ground came a bubblin' crude.
Oil That is! Black gold, Texas tea!

COURTESY OF CURT MASSEY

Curt Massey, musician extraordinaire, performed and recorded all of the background music for the show. Massey also wrote and sang the theme to "Petticoat Junction."

Well, the first thing you know, Jed's a millionaire
Kin-folk said, "Jed, move away from there." Said,
Californy is th' place y' oughta be, so they
loaded up the truck, and they moved to Beverly.
Hills that is! Swimmin' pools, Movie stars!

Ol' Jed bought a mansion, Lawdy it was swank
Next door neighbor was pres'dent of the bank,
Lotsa folks objected, but the banker found no fault,
'Cause ol' Jed's millions was a-layin in the vault
Cash, that is! Capital gains, Depletion money!

Well now it's time to say goodbye to Jed and all his kin
An' they would like t' thank you folks fer kindly droppin' in.
You're all invited back again to this locality,
T' have a heapin' helpin' of their hospitality.
Hillbilly that is! Set a spell. Take your shoes off!
Y'all come back, hear!

Copyright © 1962 by Carolintone Music Company, Inc.

Noticeably, the third verse was stricken from the theme, sung by Jerry Scoggins with music by Lester Flatt and Earl Scruggs. In 1963, an instrumental version by Flatt and Scruggs reached number forty-four on *Billboard*'s Hot 100 chart.

THE NEXT EIGHT YEARS

6:00 A.M.: Paul Henning routinely would arrive and set out coffee and doughnuts for the cast.

8:00 A.M.: Most of the cast would be ready to start work, if required that day. If this was a read-through day, they were in the office or on the set to recite their lines with the rest of the cast. The director, Henning, the cast, technicians, Frank Inn the animal trainer, and the guest cast would be present.

With one lonely camera, the rest of the episodes were filmed on 35-mm film. Rarely did they use two cameras. During the first three seasons, the show was filmed in black and white, and the behind-the-scenes action was as hectic as on the General Service soundstage. In the offices, publicity men, including Ted Switzer and Lincoln Haynes along with a variety of other agents, made their livings promoting the show and honoring requests of affiliate stations. Paul Henning spent the day writing in his office, leaving only to solve a problem on the set.

Actually, this is a description of an average day on the set, according to Phil Gordon, who played Jasper Depew in the early episodes. Gordon also became the dialogue coach and personal assistant to Henning during most of the run of the show.

PHOTO BY GABI RONA

At the time this photo was taken the show was resting comfortably in the ratings. Here, Irene, Donna, and Buddy smile for photographer Gabi Rona.

"In the morning, on shooting days, we'd sit in a circle on the set before shooting and we ran lines," says Gordon. "Then the actors would go to their own dressing rooms and study by themselves and get ready with any makeup or costumes."

Irene Ryan required the most elaborate makeup job, donning a wig, steel-toed boots, and "granny" glasses perched on the end of her nose. Max Baer and Donna Douglas had a simple wardrobe of jeans, checkered shirts, and ropes for belts. Ebsen only had to affix the fake mustache and pop on his ragged hat and coat.

Ray Bailey applied a convincing head of hair for his role as the ambitious bank president, Mr. Drysdale. Every morning he slid the well-tailored graying toupee on his dome. Anyone who didn't know him well would never suspect that the hair wasn't his own. When the toupee was off, sometimes he wasn't even recognized walking down the street. Cast members described Bailey as a "publicity monger" who loved the recognition and was upset when fans didn't recognize him.

COURTESY OF VIACOM

The famous "Granny wig" cost a whopping $500 and proved to be a good investment. Ryan owned two wigs throughout the series.

One morning as the cast prepared for the day's shooting, a peculiar clumping was heard on the soundstage. The director called, "Cut! What the hell is that noise?"

There was dead silence.

Shooting resumed only to be interrupted by the rhythmic clump, clump, clump, clump.

Finally, the origin of the noise was discovered. The boots Irene Ryan wore for her role as Granny were pounding the floor as she walked the set, and she hadn't realized how loud the sound actually was. Irene agreed to try on a different pair of boots with softer soles.

"I tried another pair one day but I couldn't seem to feel the character without those big army boots," Ryan told a *TV Guide* reporter. "They let me have them back when I promised to walk quietly."

This was not the only problem the cast and crew encountered while filming. Henning had promised the owner of the Bel-Air home that he would keep its location a secret. Just as the fourth season was about to get under way, the address was discovered and leaked to *TV Guide.*

Immediately, tourists began driving by, knocking on the owner's door asking if Jed was home. Henning describes the owner's reaction:

> She called up and complained and we had to give up location filming. The tragedy was that we were just about to go to color. This broke before we had a chance to film the exteriors

An early publicity shot taken at the cabin location in California for the pilot episode.

COURTESY OF PAUL HENNING

in color. That was a real blow. We had to promise to stay away. She had just been beleaguered by tourists. She had to get security people, shut her gates . . . it was a terrible mess.

People actually would walk into her house and ask for Granny—thinking they really lived there. Can you imagine?

The fourth year of filming was not to include any more outdoor shots of the mansion, and never again did the series use any extremely long shots of the building. But by this time, the location was well established and the public hardly noticed.

CBS had converted all of their programming to color, finally, in 1965, and the first episode to broadcast that season showing the true colors of the Hillbillies was "Admiral Jed Clampett."

Admiral Clampett had no problem with color, but Buddy Ebsen did.

"Stay out of the sun. No more tans or sunburns," was the order that Ebsen and the rest of the cast received from Harry Wolf, director of photography, as a consequence of the show's switch from black and white.

This stricture particularly affected Ebsen, who spent long hours in the sun during weekends, holidays, and vacations. He was, and still is, an avid sailor, with more than thirty racing trophies to his collection.

Ebsen had no intention of forsaking his seagoing ways, but for a while he had to squelch this activity and cultivate his pallor.

Wolf's order had to do with the complexities of the reproduction of colors by color film. If the skin coloring of the actors changed from day to day, Wolf would be obliged to "make new film tests and adjustments daily in lighting and makeup, a procedure that would consume far too much time," a CBS press release noted.

As with any successful television program, there were legal hassles. Directly after the Hillbillies hit it big, a suit against Filmways by four members of the original radio troupe entitled "The Beverly Hillbillies" sued for a whopping $2 million. They eventually settled out of court for an undisclosed but substantial amount.

No sooner did producers of the show file that case in their legal folders than another damage suit arrived. Writer Hamilton Morgan was asking a cool $15 million for theft of his "Country Cousins" script, which had previously been turned down by CBS. He claimed the similarity between "Country Cousins" and "The Beverly Hillbillies" was too great. The charges were dismissed on "jurisdictional grounds" because the case was filed in New York and the Hillbillies were conceived, shot, and distributed from the West Coast.

Without money coming in from the sponsors, the show would not have had funds to pay its exorbitant legal fees, expenses, and

COURTESY OF TED SWITZER

Ted Switzer, publicity agent for the show, out on the town with Irene Ryan and Buddy Ebsen in Hollywood.

Two early ads for Kellogg's featuring Granny and Jed pushin' their favorite vittles.

COURTESY OF KELLOGG'S

salaries. Originally, the show was sponsored by the R. J. Reynolds Tobacco Company and the Kellogg's Company. These two corporations were lucky to sign with a show that reaped a lot of mileage from successful ratings. Moreover, the cast was a willing one that went out of its way to film specialized commercials and ad campaigns for its sponsors.

The funniest of the commercials was for Winston cigarettes, before television promotion for cigarettes was banned by the surgeon general. Especially when viewed today, the commercials are extremely campy and filled with the show's own brand of Hillbilly corn. R. J. Reynolds, although a faithful sponsor, pulled its support after the surgeon general's warning.

"Even before the break, the surgeon general released a warning about the hazards of smoking," says Paul Henning. "We got together as a cast and decided we better not do any more 'cast commercials' for Winston as it would be bad publicity."

The shooting schedule for the show was hectic, cranking out one, and eventually two, episodes per week. They were usually shot in three days after a quick read-through of the script. Paul Henning would gauge by the reading if any alterations were

COURTESY OF PAUL HENNING

The birthday celebration thrown for Paul Henning encompasses cast and crew from shows filmed at General Services Studios. Note Raymond Bailey (behind left of Nancy Kulp) in glasses and minus toupee.

PHOTO BY GABI RONA

Plain Jane Hathaway: The quest
for a man never ceases for
Drysdale's Girl Friday.

necessary, and production was guided by what scene didn't need
rewriting at the time. If revisions were needed, Henning would
retreat to his office and crank out a new version of the script—
sometimes handing pages to the cast minutes before the episodes were to be shot.

Each of the cast had his or her working idiosyncrasies. Buddy
Ebsen used to sleep on the set in any old corner, chair, or nook.
He could often be found taking "power naps" between scenes.

"He'd say, 'come in my trailer and run some lines before we
shoot,'" character actor Shad Heller says. "He'd fall asleep after I
fed him a line."

Ebsen also had a Japanese man come in and cook for him
every day in his dressing room. Ebsen lived it up, and of course
he should have since he was the "big name" or star of the show,
making one of the largest salaries of the cast.

On the other hand, Max Baer kept to himself. He preferred to
follow up on his avid interest in the behind-the-scenes aspect of
the filming, which years later resulted in several highly successful motion picture productions to his credit.

"One time Irene and I were on the set and Max came up to us
excitedly," says Nancy Kulp. "He started explaining this movie

he'd seen the night before, and he went into great detail about the shots, angles, and such. Irene and I kept nudging each other, but he just rattled on. Finally we got called for the scene. But a little later he came up and started on that bit again and talked us to death. He really has an eye for direction and how a picture should move."

Donna Douglas, who played the beautiful Elly May, was cordial, sensitive, and very easy to get along with. She required little or no direction regarding her character—she *was* Elly. Donna spent hours autographing photos and responding to her voluminous mail.

"She was very conscientious," says director Joe Depew. "It was impossible to photograph Donna from an angle that made her look bad."

After one series hiatus, the whole cast and crew noticed a complete change in Donna. She had become quiet and passive. While members of the cast tried to bring her out, Donna remained withdrawn.

It seems that during her break in filming, she costarred with Elvis Presley in the movie *Frankie and Johnnie*. Some of the cast and her working associates intimated that she fell in love and

COURTESY OF UNITED ARTISTS

Some said Douglas fell in love with Elvis after starring opposite the King in *Frankie and Johnny* in 1966. She returned to the Hillbillies set heartbroken.

COURTESY OF GEORGE FABER

Raymond Bailey with a genuine smile was rarely seen. To the Hillbillies cast he was a publicity monger.

was completely consumed with the king of rock 'n' roll. "She didn't realize every girl he worked with fell in love with him plus a million he didn't work with," says Paul Henning. "She really flipped out."

Director Joe Depew remembers how this infatuation affected filming: "In the film [*Frankie and Johnnie*], she shoots Johnnie. When she came back to work, we had a sequence where she had to handle a pistol. She couldn't do it. She said to me finally, 'Look, I can't do this. I've asked Paul and he's gonna let me hold a rifle.' She wouldn't hold a gun, and I think [the gun incident] had something to do with it."

Douglas, when asked about this period, said: "I wouldn't interpret it as love or infatuation, but I was going through a rough time in my life then."

Raymond Bailey, the boisterous member of the cast, was brash and rude and would argue about anything, according to the cast. Remembers Ruth Henning, Paul's wife:

"We were going to a bank opening in Independence, Missouri, where Paul grew up," Mrs. Henning says of a trip with Bailey, Nancy Kulp, and her husband. "He got loaded on the plane and when we arrived at Paul's sister's house, a big, historical, Victorian-style home, Ray made a loud remark that it looked like a whorehouse. When Paul's sister stepped out on the porch to greet us, Ray said, 'Are you the madam?' "

Kulp remembers Raymond Bailey spotting her name above his on a call sheet one day and becoming "livid." "He became incensed when he saw that. I was usually listed as number six on the totem pole, but that day for some reason I wasn't. But then again, he was livid most of the time."

Director Depew said, "You just couldn't take Ray seriously. He got mad at an ostrich on the set one time. Ray got so damn mad because the ostrich wouldn't hit his mark that he threw a punch at it!"

HILLBILLY LINGO . . . IN ONE EASY LESSON

Corse youns would hear what the Clampetts was a' sayin' on all them there programs ever' week. They talked in th' hillbilly language o' the Ozarks. Here, in one easy lessun, youns can pick up a few o' them werds sose ya' know what we're yappin 'bout. Study up, now!

Frequently Used Phrases:

"Set a spell."
" . . . feelin' lower than a well-digger's heel." (sickly)
"Ya tucked yer tail betwixt yer legs, didn't ya?"
"I'll commence ta fixin' the vittles."
"Err ya gonna spark her, Jed?" (kiss)
"Ya got slickered an ya shamed t' amit it."

In fact, writer Paul Henning wrote the scripts to appear just like that. The actors were required to learn the lines to the syllable, unless Paul gave the word, so to speak.

Lingo T' Teach Them Goomers

Ainjun—Jethro cain't ever fix the truck's ainjun.
Argy—Elly don't argy with Jed, 'coze he's her paw.
Ast—Jethro ast Granny fer more vittles.
Banch—Jed has a banch in his workshop, yonder.
Bar—Did you find a cash bar (buyer) for th' farm?
Bobbed—Don't tear yore britches on that bobbed war (wire).
Bubs—The light bubs burned out.
Californy—A far west state where there ain't no snow.

Canny—Let Jethrine have a peeny's wuth of that rock canny.

Cheer—Granny sits in th' rockin' cheer sometimes.

Commence—start or begin.

Coze—We cain't go to tyown Satidy coze we're havin' dinner at home.

Daintz—Granny likes to square daintz.

Dar—Destitute; They're in dar need.

Dawk—Granny's profession, a doctor (Doc).

Dreckly—Right away; Fetch the truck dreckly, Jethro!

Eench—twelve eenches to a foot.

Et—Jethro et all his dinner—an' then some!

Fark—Knife, spoon, and fark.

Fer—for.

Ferener—foreigners; Fereners aren't welcome 'round moonshiners.

Flar—A rose is about the purdiest flar Granny done seen.

Ford—Foreword; Granny says Jethro best come ford if he et the grits.

Gay-us—Put some gay-us in the tank, Jethro.

Grain—A color; Granny was grain with envy of Elverna Bradshaw.

Goomers—Dummies or oddballs.

Hep—Elly cain't hep it; critters just a' foller her 'round.

Heerd—He ain't heerd a word ya said.

Hern—It ain't hern, it's hisn.

Hillbilly—Somebody else.

Hit—If that don't beat all, don't hit?

Int—Int Elly's pet skunk a cute ol' thing?

Jist—Jist a dadgummed minute there, stranger.

Kag—A container; kag o' beer, kag o' nails.

Lack—Jethrine was lack her brother Jethro—big!

Lar—Fightin' word used for someone not telllin' the truth. "Billy Bob is a damlar."

Mess—A bunch; Granny 'll fix a mess o' greens.

Mull—Think; Jed 'll mull it over before he decides.

New-monie—A lung ailment, more serious than a varrus (virus).

Nup—A hillbilly's "no!"

Orl—The truck needs two quarts orl.

Pawpaw—A native fruit kin to papaya.

Pie-annie—Cousin Pearl played the pie-annie at the local theater in Bug Tussle.

Polecat—A skunk.

Purdy—Elly May sure is purdy in a dress.

Raid—A bright color; She had raid hair.

Seed—He seed her first.

Sofy—What you an' yore girl spark on in the parlor. (sofa)

Spark—Kiss.

Thanks—Jethro thanks he's so smart.

Trappins—Clothes; Jed's got fancy trappins to go courtin'.

Turble—Granny thinks folks out here are turble.

Twixt—(Also betwixt); Between.

Varmits—What Granny called Elly's critters.

Walled—Wild; Elly May is a walled deer.

Wil par—Jethro has no wil par when it comes t' vittles.

Worsh—Elly May bathed in a worsh tub.

X—How some hillbillies sign their name.

Younguns—The young ones: Elly May and Jethro.

Yore—Your.

Yurp—The continent overseas.

2
CAST BIOGRAPHIES

BUDDY EBSEN
Jed Clampett

Christian Ebsen, Jr.—that's his name, not religious description—turns eighty this year and doesn't mind boasting that he's started another decade. His skin is reddened from his outdoor life and his hair has turned white. But even from across the room, you can recognize the face. Well Doggies, it's Jed Clampett!

The patriarchal Clampett doesn't have much to say about the nine years spent playing TV's number one hillbilly. He's writing his own book now, tentatively called *The Other Side of Oz*, referring to his original casting as the Tin Man in the MGM classic, *The Wizard of Oz*. Unfortunately, he fell ill due to the poisonous silver makeup used, which infected his eyes and lungs, and was unable to finish the role.

"Jed is a part of America now," Ebsen says. "There's a resurgence of popularity for the Hillbillies, and I'd like to capitalize on that. In my own selfish way, I want to keep the anecdotes for my own book. Fans don't want to read the same story twice." He did, however, verify some important background information.

Ebsen was born in 1908 in Belleville, Illinois, and grew up in Orlando, Florida, where he moved with his family when he was twelve.

Although his father owned a dancing school, young Ebsen spurned dancing lessons. He went to the University of Florida and Rollins College to study pre-med. Then he changed his mind about dancing. He went to New York and won his first Broadway role as a dancer in the 1928 Ziegfeld production of

PHOTO BY GABI RONA

Whoopee with Eddie Cantor. His sister, Vilma, became his dancing partner, and for several years the team of Vilma and Buddy Ebsen drew attention in nightclub engagements, on road tours, and in a string of musicals culminating with *Flying Colors*, a top revue of 1932.

Ebsen then moved to Hollywood, where stars were under contract and the lights shone brightly on the screen legends of the era. His dancing graced such films as *Lucky Star*, *Captain January* with Shirley Temple, and *Broadway Melody of 1938*.

He even tackled songwriting and found immediate success with "Baby Blues," "Squeezin' Polka," and "I'll See You." But acting took precedence, and he appeared in dramas such as *Breakfast at Tiffany's* and *Night People*, among many others.

Ebsen's career in television started off well. He played the rough-and-ready sidekick of Davy Crockett (played by Fess Parker) in the Walt Disney series. Then along came the role of Jed Clampett, which creator Paul Henning had written with Ebsen in mind.

Buddy spent many hours in jeans, a tan coat, and raggedy hat, with spirit gum dabbed on his upper lip to support his false mustache. On the set of the Hillbillies, when not practicing a tap-dance sequence or two, he usually retreated to an available chair or corner and fell asleep between takes.

"He's got the marvelous ability to sit down and catnap anywhere, anytime," says Hillbilly director Joe Depew. "That's what kept him going all those years. Bob Hope was that way, too. Sometimes it would be hard to walk over and say, Buddy, I hate to do this, baby, but we're on."

Buddy may have slept offscreen, but on-screen his performance never made viewers snooze. He went almost directly into

Ebsen's first
dance partner
was his sister, Vilma.

COURTESY OF BUDDY EBSEN

COURTESY OF VIACOM

PHOTO BY STEPHEN COX

Buddy Ebsen at age eighty, in 1988.

another series after the Hillbillies, in which he portrayed Barnaby Jones, private investigator. Because of his many television successes, he doesn't feel he has been stereotyped.

"When Buddy was at the London Palladium and the Hillbillies were the top show in England," says Hillbillies publicity man Ted Switzer, "he did an act where he danced, sang a little. And then he said, 'Maybe there's a character you folks know me from.' Then a beautiful showgirl brought out the Jed hat on a purple velvet pillow. Buddy turned his back and put it on. Then he faced the audience and said, 'Well Doggies!,' set the hat back, and resumed his show. The audience went wild. They loved it."

Outside of acting, Buddy loves politics, literature, and United States history, even to the extent of portraying Abraham Lincoln in a stage play. He is a handy man around his home in Long Beach and a fisherman and expert sailor. His catamaran, *Polynesian Concept*, keeps him out on the water and exposed to the sun. He and his third wife, Dorothy, enjoy life near the beach, and Buddy occasionally takes an acting role or gives a personal appearance. He's comfortable with his life after three successful series.

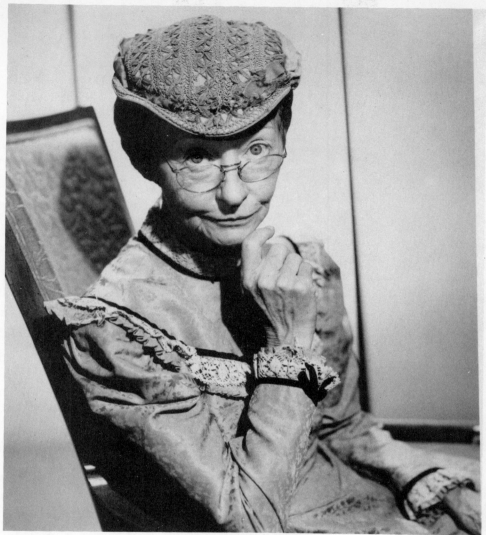

COURTESY OF VIACOM

IRENE RYAN
Granny

Irene was everyone's favorite.
—Paul Henning

If there ever was an actress who enjoyed a role, it was Irene Ryan, the wispy little woman who endearingly portrayed one of television's most memorable characters—Granny.

Having worked since childhood, Irene dabbled in just about every medium show business had to offer. She was trained in the "old school" of entertainment, learning early how to project to

Irene Ryan in her pre-Granny days.

COURTESY OF IRENE RYAN COLLECTION

the back of the theater and belt out a tune so every note could be heard. She became a show-business institution during her struggle to the top and finally made it with her role as Daisy Moses, Granny.

Irene was born in El Paso, Texas, on October 17, 1902, and at an early age moved to San Francisco with her parents, Sgt. James and Kathleen Noblette. She began her show business career at a tender eleven years old, singing "Pretty Baby" at an amateur contest on the stage of San Francisco's old Valencia Theater. Irene became a vaudeville headliner and toured across the country when still in her teens. From vaudeville, she stepped into radio, appearing with Meredith Willson on "Carefree Carnival" in 1932. This led to appearances on "The Rudy Vallee Show," "The Jack Carson Show," and Bob Hope's popular radio program. At one point, she and her new husband, Tim Ryan, starred in the popular "Tim and Irene Ryan Show."

The success of radio was a springboard to motion pictures (including *Desire in the Dust*, *Bonzo Goes to College*, and *Diary of a Chambermaid*). In between stints at movie studios, Irene performed a nightclub act. Then divorced from Tim she worked as a single in clubs across America.

Doris Day, Bob Hope, and Irene Ryan on tour for the troops in Berlin, 1948.

COURTESY OF KINGSLEY COLTON

COURTESY OF BOB HOPE

Bob Hope: "The word 'delight' pops up when I think of Irene Ryan. She was a wonderful gal with a great sense of timing; she was a delight and always made me happy."

When Bob Hope toured military installations during World War II, he asked his pal Irene to join him. She soon became known as "the gal who makes Bob Hope laugh." In their famous Christmas Caravan, with Hope, Irene, Doris Day, and the Les Brown Orchestra, they toured Germany, where they entertained U.S. airmen of the Berlin airlift before returning to the states to visit thirty-five leading cities.

Reenie, as friends called her, worked hard in film and on stage, and when television lightened America, she made appearances on "The Dennis Day Show," "Make Room for Daddy," "Comedy House," and "All-Star Revue," to name a few. In 1962, she struck oil in her career when she won her role as Granny.

Henning clearly remembers when he first discussed the role with Irene, a tiny lady who stood 5'2" tall and weighed 100 pounds.

"I said, 'Tell me, Irene, do you think you could play a hillbilly character?' " Henning says. "She said, 'Oh yes . . . when I was in

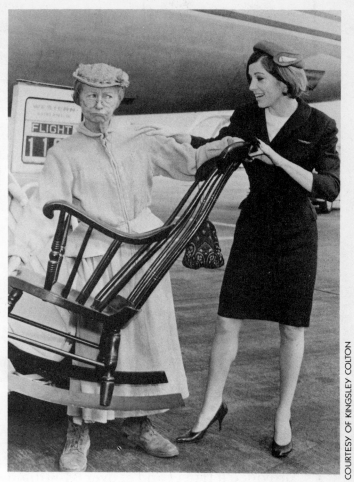

Under all those prim prairie outfits and steel-toed boots . . . we never realized! This studio gag shot melded Granny's head with an early starlet's voluptuous figure.

Commuting daily for four weeks between series filming in Hollywood and her Las Vegas show at the Sahara Hotel got to be tiring. Every day Ryan rushed in costume and makeup from the studio to board a Western Airlines flight bound for the gamblin' town to perform with Donald O'Connor to sell-out crowds.

stock company, we played a little theater in rural Arkansas. We were waiting for the curtain to go up, and we knew there were people outside waiting to get in, and the manager wouldn't let them in.

"We asked, 'why don't you let the people in?' He said, 'I can't let them in until you're ready to take up the curtain, 'else if I do, they'll sit there and whittle the seats away!'"

After she got the role of Granny, she revered it, milked it, and molded the character into a household word. "She could never eat dinner out," says her agent Kingsley Colton. "She was mobbed everywhere.

COURTESY OF KINGSLEY COLTON

Kingsley Colton, Irene Ryan's agent, escorts her to the premiere of *The Americanization of Emily*, starring Julie Andrews. (1964)

"Nothing fazed her—that's why she was as great as she was. She was always kind to her fans—always!"

After the cancellation of "The Beverly Hillbillies," Irene established a scholarship fund in gratitude to her profession. She provided a trust fund of over $1 million to award thirteen annual scholarships to the outstanding theater arts students throughout the country in conjunction with the American College Theater Festival. The Irene Ryan Scholarship program was inaugurated on April 23, 1972, at the John F. Kennedy Center for the Performing Arts in Washington, D.C. Today the program is under the guidance of the executor of her estate, Kingsley Colton.

After Hillbillies, Irene costarred in Bob Fosse's *Pippin*, starring Ben Vereen and a group of other big names. She had received rave reviews portraying the lusty grandmother, Bertha, when a few months into the show, Irene suffered what newspapers called a stroke while performing in the show's Saturday matinee.

She died of a brain tumor a few weeks later, on April 26, 1973. She was seventy-one.

On the morning of Friday, April 27, the *Los Angeles Times* ran a large, bold headline above its masthead: IRENE RYAN, TV 'GRANNY,' DIES AT 71. The word *Granny*, recognized as only one person, was all that was needed.

The services for Irene Ryan were held on Tuesday, May 1, 1973,

COURTESY OF RALPH EDWARDS PRODUCTIONS

Ryan is shown here with Ralph Edwards at the Movieland Wax Museum in Buena Park, California, where she went ostensibly to unveil a "Beverly Hillbillies" exhibit. Friends Meredith Wilson, Arthur Lake, Buddy Ebsen, Donna Douglas, and Paul Henning were on hand to pay tribute to Ryan on "This Is Your Life."

at 2:30 P.M. in Santa Monica, California. Serving as Irene's pallbearers were Max Baer, Kingsley Colton, Buddy Ebsen, Ralph Handley, Paul Henning, and Edward Sherman. Honorary pallbearers included Bob Hope, Bob Fosse, Al Simon, and Ben Vereen.

Paul Henning was asked to perform two uneasy tasks that day. Besides being a pallbearer, he delivered the eulogy, here, in part.

Today is May first. May Day. Mayday—the international distress signal. And that's exactly what the death of Irene Ryan brought about . . . a universal feeling of distress because she was known and loved all over the world. . . .

Yes, this is indeed a time to cry. Mayday! Help! We're in

COURTESY OF KINGSLEY COLTON

One of the last photographs taken of Irene Ryan, pictured here in her costume for Bob Fosse's *Pippin*. Ryan was not aware that she was suffering from a brain tumor.

distress! But May Day has another meaning . . . a much older meaning. Long before it became a call for help, May Day was a time of joy and celebration. And I think that's the meaning Reenie would want us to have in our hearts today. Because if anyone ever had a full, rich, joyous life, it was Irene Ryan. What could possibly be more fulfilling than to achieve success. A towering success! . . .

If you knew her, and I assume that everyone here did, you know that you simply could not be gloomy around Irene. She was always the life of the party, or rehearsal, or whatever gathering it might be. She saw to it that everyone had a good time. And she had the best time of all. She had a marvelous life! . . .

Reenie once told me that there was an old saying in vaudeville—I guess it applies to all of show business. "Always get off at the high point of your act. Leave 'em wanting more." Well, Irene, you certainly made your exit at a high point. God knows we wanted more!

DONNA DOUGLAS
Elly May Clampett

Sparkling Donna Douglas was born Doris Smith in Baywood, Louisiana, on September 26, coincidentally the same day "The Beverly Hillbillies" premiered on CBS in 1962. That was an extremely happy birthday for Donna, as the show catapulted her to recognition as one of the most beautiful girls in show business—or any business.

PHOTO BY GABI RONA

Donna Douglas
"Elly May"

She won't divulge her age, although it's estimated she's in her mid-fifties; but her appearance has scarcely changed. She was Elly May in the sixties, and she remains Elly May. She radiates a glow men swoon over, although when she was young, she was the tomboy of the neighborhood.

"I was a real tomboy, but it was a matter of survival," she recalls. "I was the only girl on either side of my family and I was surrounded by boys—an older brother and eight cousins, all boys." At an early age, she learned to jump off woodsheds, hunt, fish, and play football, basketball, baseball, and softball. "I was a pitcher on the boys' softball team for so long I was fourteen before I found out there was a girls' team."

Like the character she made famous, Douglas grew up loving nature and has always remained especially fond of animals. She credits her understanding of Elly to the simplicity of her childhood in rural Louisiana. "I'd never trade anything for the summers we used to spend on my granddaddy's place," she says. "They let me ride the horses and feed the pigs and taught me how to milk the cows with both hands."

COURTESY OF HOWARD FRANK ARCHIVES

"Merry Christmas from the critters and me!"

When Douglas blossomed into her teens, she began cheerleading and winning beauty contests. She was awarded the Miss Baton Rouge title and then became Miss New Orleans of 1957. Her success in these contests took her to New York, where she appeared as the Letters Girl on "The Perry Como Show" and a Billboard Girl on "The Steve Allen Show."

Douglas guested on a variety of television shows before auditioning for the role of Elly May. Her movie credits include *Li'l Abner* and *Frankie and Johnny*, the movie in which she played opposite Elvis Presley. She also had a role in the movie *Lover Come Back*, written by Paul Henning. This was her first meeting with the man who later put her at the top of the idol list in the sixties with her role as Elly May Clampett.

"Right when it [Hillbillies] hit big, I was at home and my dad came home one night . . . everybody was so excited by the success of the show," Douglas says. "And my folks are kind of laid-back, quiet people. They are basic and don't make a fuss over everything. They don't know that much about Hollywood.

"My dad went out to the store and came back. When he came in he said, 'You know what? Somebody called me Jed Clampett.' It was so precious!"

Douglas always made sure she did her bit for promotion of the show, which she was proud of. During its run, she traveled to

Rickshaw Racin': Donna Douglas on her tour of Japan as a guest of Sanyo Electronics.

PHOTO BY GEORGE FABER

An advertisement for Donna Douglas's arrival in Japan.

COURTESY OF PAUL HENNING

PHOTO BY STEPHEN COX

Donna Douglas in 1988.

Japan and Australia to greet fans and talk about Elly May and, of course, receive honors. "That's the responsibility of success," she says. "The fans are the ones that put you there."

When the show began, Douglas was recently divorced and had custody of her only son, Danny (who is now thirty-six). Donna's second marriage, to Hillbillies director Robert Leeds, ended in divorce around 1980.

Currently, Douglas spends her time traveling and is working on her second gospel album. She loves to work with young people and speaks frequently at church groups. "I care about young people," she says. "You can't just receive; you have to give back."

Douglas still loves to be recognized as Elly May and makes two or three annual appearances around the United States, still dressed in the familiar pink checkered shirt and rope-tied jeans. She can still belt out a whistle through her teeth with a shrill blast that could peel the bark off a cottonwood tree at three hundred paces.

MAX BAER
Jethro Bodine

If you're wondering how big Jethro really is, all you have to do is look at actor Max Baer.

Baer weighs 210 pounds and is 6'4". He has brown hair and hazel eyes. Like his father, world heavyweight boxing champion, Max Baer, Sr., he has an avid interest in sports.

Baer was born on December 4, 1937, and at the age of three

PHOTO BY GABI RONA

moved with his parents to Sacramento, California, where he grew up and attended Christian Brothers High School. There, he channeled his energy into athletics, winning letters in golf, football, baseball, and basketball. He also won the Sacramento Junior Open Golf Championship two years in a row, later taking the runner-up title in the men's tournament.

Baer's interest in show business began during his days in high school and at the University of Santa Clara, where he studied and received his bachelor's degree in business administration with a minor in philosophy. He won letters there in boxing and golf and performed in his first play, a student production of *The Male Animal.*

After graduation, Baer served in the Air Force for six months

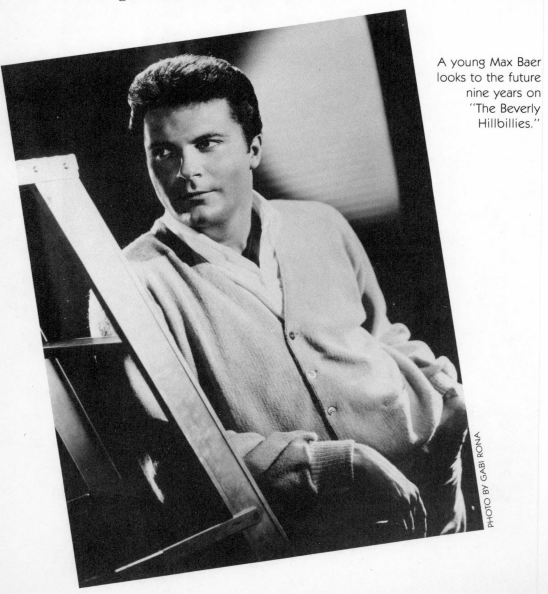

A young Max Baer looks to the future nine years on "The Beverly Hillbillies."

PHOTO BY GABI RONA

COURTESY OF MAX BAER

Max Baer in his 1974 hit movie, *Macon County Line*, which he wrote and produced after not finding work for three years.

before going to Hollywood to pursue an acting career. He appeared in more than twenty television productions before landing his role as Jethro, one he thought he wouldn't receive. "Max was the only one who could have played Jethro," recalls creator Paul Henning. "Nobody could have done it better, I'm convinced. He was great."

Before landing the role, Baer was not very healthy, physically or financially: "I was two months behind in my rent, and my weight had dropped from 210 to 188 pounds," he remembers. That changed quickly upon signing the contract to star in "The Beverly Hillbillies."

Baer costarred in *The Long Ride Home* with Glenn Ford, George Hamilton, and Inger Stevens, while still playing Jethro in the series. After the Hillbillies, Max, who couldn't find work in Hollywood because he was associated with the show, solved his problem by making his own movie, *Macon County Line*, which proved to be an enormous success. Max wrote, produced, and starred in this dramatic feature, released in 1974.

Baer's 1975 sequel, *Return to Macon County*, which starred Don Johnson and Nick Nolte, was an unworthy attempt to refuel the success of the first movie.

Baer's recent television appearances have been few, but they

COURTESY OF MARK GILMAN

Max Baer, still the athletic type in 1988.

include "Fantasy Island," and "Matt Houston," the latter of which reunited Max with his old costar, Buddy Ebsen.

Currently Baer is working on two films, which he expects will begin production in late 1988. He collaborated on the screenplay for one of the films, and is not sure whether he will once again step in front of the camera for these projects.

RAYMOND BAILEY
Milburn Drysdale

As a young man, Raymond Bailey aspired to be a banker or a stockbroker, but after he worked in the field, he deserted high finance for a career in show business. Ironically, many years later, he would become America's most famous banker and cheapskate. The road between his two careers was a long one,

PHOTO BY GABI RONA

Raymond Bailey

taking him around the world several times and into many lines of work.

Bailey was born in San Francisco on May 6, 1905. Not much is known about his childhood until after high school, when Bailey moved to Hollywood and landed a job as a laborer at a movie studio. He hoped to be discovered by a director or producer, but instead he was fired for attempting to sneak into a mob scene. He then hitchhiked to New York to try a stage career, but had no luck.

Young Bailey, "penniless and hungry" as his CBS biography reports, "shipped out as a mess boy on a freighter bound for San

Francisco." He spent the next few years at sea as a deck hand, seaman, and quartermaster, traveling to China, Japan, the Philippines, Hawaii, and the Mediterranean.

During the Depression, he attempted to tackle Hollywood once again but without success. He worked for a variety of employers, including a pineapple plantation and a shipping firm. While in Hawaii, he worked in community theater. That led to a few traveling roles in stock companies. When Bailey returned to Hollywood, he continued the bit parts and in 1938, he launched his film career at Warner Brothers Studios with, as he put it, "several unspectacular parts in several unspectacular movies." His initial role was in *Blackwell Island* with John Garfield.

Ray's more important movie credits include roles in *Picnic*, *No Time for Sergeants*, and *Al Capone*. He also successfully tackled Broadway starring in productions such as *The Bat*, *Mister Roberts*, and *The Caine Mutiny Court Martial*, among others.

Bailey also performed in more than three hundred television shows, including "My Sister Eileen" and "Dobie Gillis," before winning the role of the scheming Mr. Drysdale on "The Beverly Hillbillies." Between seasons he appeared in theater productions.

Ray and his wife, the former Gaby George of Sydney, Australia, lived in Laguna Niguel, California, until his death on April 15, 1980, of a heart attack at the age of seventy-four.

COURTESY OF 20TH CENTURY-FOX

Myrna Loy, Raymond Bailey, Paul Newman, and Joanne Woodward in *From the Terrace* (1960).

COURTESY OF NOLAND ROAD BANK

Drysdale Dollars: Raymond Bailey took delight in passing out these specially printed bills and autographing them for fans. These are now rare collector's items among aficionados of the show.

Bailey, according to most of the cast, was somewhat hard to work with. "He wasn't happy anywhere he was," says Paul Henning who hired him for the Drysdale role. "He complained a lot, but he played the part perfectly." He had a temper that would flare in an instant and calm in a flash. Many times on the set of "The Beverly Hillbillies," he would muddle his lines and get very angry. Nancy Kulp, who probably worked the most with him on the set, explains what her moody cohort was like:

"He called me 'Slim' all the time. He would blow up and I would try and calm him down and then he'd be OK. I seemed to be able to do that most of the time.

"I visited Bailey after the series was canceled at his home in Laguna Niguel. At first when he saw me, his eyes lit up. Then he said, 'Oh, it's you, Slim.' He liked me, but rarely showed it. And when I talked with him then, he was wondering why he wasn't getting any work. He talked for a half hour about negative things and griped about everything.

"God, he was aggravating, but I'd just say, 'Yes, Raymond, yes. . . .' That was the way to handle him. When he'd blow up, people got so used to it, they just accepted it as normal."

Shortly after his death, *The National Enquirer* published a story about Bailey headlined: BEVERLY HILLBILLIES COSTAR DIES LONELY, SHUNNED BY BUDDY EBSEN. The article detailed how, after the series ended, Ebsen did not offer work to Bailey in his series "Barnaby Jones." It was reported that this had made Bailey extremely bitter in his last years after his success in the role of Milburn Drysdale.

"He alienated himself from everybody," says Don Richardson, a press agent who worked with Bailey. "Sometimes people hated to be around him, he complained so much."

Buddy Ebsen found Bailey "entertaining," on the other hand. "He was always good for a laugh."

Drysdale arouses Granny's sympathy when he pretends insanity by posing as Napoleon.

COURTESY OF VIACOM

NANCY KULP
Miss Jane Hathaway

Nancy Kulp was born in Harrisburg, Pennsylvania, on August 28, "A.D.," she says. During her childhood, Kulp attended seventeen schools in Pennsylvania, eventually settling in Florida, after her father bought a private school in Miami Beach.

Kulp received her bachelor's degree in journalism from Florida State University and studied for her master's degree in English at the University of Miami. She had aspirations to have a career in newscasting. "Of course television was in its infancy," she says. "And women had no place in television journalism at the time. I'd love to be in the field today."

In 1951, Kulp left Florida and headed for the equally warm climate of Hollywood, where casting director Billy Gordon and director George Cukor thought she belonged in front of the camera instead of in the publicity business—her occupation at the time. She was given a featured role in the movie *The Model and the Marriage Broker* only three weeks after her arrival in town. Subsequent television shows during those early days of her career include "I Love Lucy," "The Red Skelton Show," "December Bride," "Playhouse 90," and five appearances on "Matinee Theater."

She has appeared in numerous motion pictures (*Shane, The Three Faces of Eve, The Night of the Grizzly, Sabrina*) and television; the two longest-running series she acted in, "The Bob

PHOTO BY GABI RONA

COURTESY OF FILMWAYS

Nancy Kulp, an avid football fan, escorts some players and a guest around the back lot of General Service Studios. Ray Bailey looks as if he would rather be somewhere else, but he always obliged photographers if there might be publicity attached.

Cummings Show" and "The Beverly Hillbillies," were both created by Henning.

From 1955 to 1959, Nancy starred as Bob's bird-watcher friend, Pamela Livingstone. In 1962 she was given the role as Miss Jane Hathaway in "The Beverly Hillbillies" (for which she received an Emmy Award nomination), and she remained with the show until its cancellation in 1971.

Following the Hillbillies, she performed throughout the country in various dinner theaters and has guested on such shows as "Love Boat," "Simon and Simon," "Fantasy Island," and "Scarecrow and Mrs. King." And Broadway welcomed Nancy in 1982 in *Mornings at Seven*.

In 1984, Kulp finally ran unsuccessfully for Congress on the Democratic ticket (House of Representatives: Ninth Congressional District in Pennsylvania). Her campaign led to a well-publicized confrontation with Buddy Ebsen. Kulp, a Democrat, and Ebsen, a Republican, had always squabbled about politics on "The Beverly Hillbillies" set. But Kulp's campaign made their differences of opinion public.

Kulp had been sinking her life savings and more into winning

the election. It seems the media aired a detrimental radio advertisement opposing Kulp, made by none other than Buddy Ebsen.
According to both parties, they have not spoken to each other
since the incident. The actors have this to say about their famous
falling-out:

Buddy Ebsen: You see, on national television, Nancy in-
ferred that all the Hillbillies supported her. Well . . . I, of
course, didn't. I did a thirty-second audio tape that opposed

"Pamela Livingstone—as I live and
breathe." This regular role of a
bird-watcher on "The Bob
Cummings Show" was
Kulp's favorite.

COURTESY OF
HOWARD FRANK ARCHIVES

COURTESY OF VIACOM

Miss Jane, disguised as Jed, is confronted by the real Jed. Today Ebsen and Kulp are at odds with each other in real life, due to political and personal differences.

her and gave it to her opponent, Bud Shuster. For years, we had had political arguments. I enjoyed them. I still do. But she was lining up endorsements from Ed Asner and other actors and I didn't think that was fair. In fact, I wrote her and commended her on the campaign, but I said I didn't feel her opponent had national profile, so I made the tape.

Nancy Kulp: I just think it was unnecessary. I haven't talked to him since. What would I say? Thanks? He needled me for ten years and he's still doing it after the show. I lost the election and it was the year of the Reagan landslide, of course, but his little bit didn't help. My opponent finally yanked the commercial because it was so inappropriate. I was infuriated with what he did! He was a great Jed, don't get me wrong. A great actor, but what right does he think he has?

Nancy Kulp in the middle of the cluttered Fred Sanford domain on "Sanford and Son," where she guest-starred during one season.

The argument between Kulp and Ebsen was real, not a publicity stunt. And though it hasn't hurt either actor's popularity, fans remember it and still ask them about it.

Following this unhappy defeat, Kulp became an Artist in Residence at Juniata College in Huntingdon, Pennsylvania. She appeared in 1987 as the nurse in *Romeo and Juliet* for Georgia's Shakespeare Festival in Atlanta. Immediately afterward, she flew to London, where she reprised the role that Edna May Oliver originated in the musical *Showboat* (Captain Andy's wife, Parthy Ann Hawks) for an album.

Nancy lives in Palm Springs, California, and serves on the Board of Directors for the Screen Actors Guild and, as you can tell, loves to stay busy. She was married once ("On and off for ten years," she says), to Charles Dacus, who she credits as helping

COURTESY OF NANCY KULP

Nancy Kulp in 1988.

her cultivate an acting career. She divorced prior to the Hillbillies series and has remained single since.

Nancy, who hasn't changed much in her appearance since she played the man-seeking, efficient secretary, is constantly questioned about her role. She delights in talking about the show and especially about her close friend, Irene Ryan.

BEA BENADERET
Cousin Pearl Bodine

When "The Beverly Hillbillies" first aired, it almost became the Bea Benaderet Show; every scene with crazy Cousin Pearl was practically stolen by actress Bea Benaderet.

Born in New York on April 4, 1906, Benaderet and her parents moved to San Francisco when she was five. She made her first radio appearance at twelve, singing in a children's production of *The Beggar's Opera*. Bea was discovered by Orson Welles, who made her a regular on the radio show "Campbell Playhouse."

PHOTO BY GABI RONA

COURTESY OF VIACOM

The cast of "Petticoat Junction,"
starring Bea Benaderet.

In her early career, Benaderet played every radio show imagin-
able, from Gertrude Gearshift, Jack Benny's Brooklyn telephone
operator, to Mrs. Carstairs on "The Fibber McGee and Molly
Show." She landed the radio role of Blanche Morton, the wacky
neighbor to George Burns and Gracie Allen on the show bearing
their names. When the program went to television in 1950, Bea
followed right along and proved as mighty an actress on the
television screen as on radio. Now, audiences who were emerging
from the radio era into the TV years could place the familiar voice
with the face. Bea appeared on other TV shows, such as "Peter
Loves Mary," and during her days of the Hillbillies and her
starring role on "Petticoat Junction" she voiced the role of Betty
Rubble on "The Flintstones" from 1960 to 1964.

The role of Pearl on the Hillbillies was given to her by possibly
her biggest fan. Paul Henning had Bea in mind for a lead in the

Cousin Pearl makes an
entrance comin' down the new-fangled movin'
stairs at the airport as she arrives in Los Angeles.

COURTESY OF FILMWAYS

show but cast her in the role of Cousin Pearl instead. "She was a
dedicated performer," Henning says. "She got herself a coach
and studied hillbilly accents. She was wonderful!"

Benaderet was married twice and had two children from her
first marriage, Jack (Bannon, also an actor, who starred in "Lou
Grant") and Maggie. But she loved acting and devoted almost her
entire life to the profession. Her work was always praised by fans,
although her talent as a comedienne, voice expert, and actress
remains underrated by critics. When she died on October 13,
1968, of cancer, the business lost one of its most versatile performers.

COURTESY OF JEAN JENSON

Harriet MacGibbon at age seventeen, the year of her stage debut.

HARRIET MACGIBBON
Mrs. Margaret Drysdale

Harriet MacGibbon was a natural scene stealer, a skill she learned at an early age. She debuted on the professional stage at the age of seventeen and first appeared on Broadway in *Beggar on Horseback*, starring Spring Byington.

This early performance paved the way for MacGibbon to gain more experience in the theater in productions like *Anniversary Waltz*, *Ladies in the Corridor*, and *The Front Page*, all performed while she was still under thirty. Her favorite role was that of Mary, the mother of Jesus, in *The Woman at the Tomb*.

MacGibbon was born on October 5, 1905, in Chicago, Illinois, an only child of a physician. She was a great-grandchild of Dr. Elisha Deming, an Indiana physician who was active in the underground railroad movement assisting slaves to flee to the North before the Civil War.

MacGibbon's family settled in New York, a natural locale for her interest in theater to develop. She completed her education at

COURTESY OF COLUMBIA PICTURES

Harriet MacGibbon in a scene from her motion picture debut in *Cry for Happy* with Donald O'Connor (left), Joe Flynn, and Glenn Ford in 1960.

the Knox School in Cooperstown, New York, and her early ambition was to be an opera singer. She studied voice, piano, and harp and planned to attend Vassar, but after appearing in a school play, she changed her mind. Harriet was an actress.

Besides Broadway performances, Harriet appeared on many early television and radio dramas. MacGibbon confined her professional activities mostly to New York until the late 1950s.

Harriet Elizabeth, which she was called by some of her friends and relatives, was married twice. Her first marriage, to William Reno Kane, ended in divorce; they had one son, William MacGibbon Kane. Her second marriage was to Charles Corwin White, who died in the mid-1970s.

During her years on the Hillbillies as the brassy, snooty Mrs. Drysdale, she also guested on other TV shows such as "Dr. Kildare," "Hennessey," "My Three Sons," "The Smothers Brothers Show," "Dragnet," and "The Ann Sothern Show." She also appeared in such motion pictures as *Four Horsemen of the Apocalypse*, *The Absent-Minded Professor*, and *Son of Flubber*.

Although her work was limited after "The Beverly Hillbillies," Harriet, a jovial, fun-loving type, enjoyed being remembered for the series. She performed in commercials and small television

COURTESY OF JEAN JENSON

Harriet E. Mae Hedson

cameos, but retired in the seventies and eighties for health reasons.

"She gained an awful lot of weight in the last few years of her life," Jean Jensen says of her cousin. "But she didn't care; she felt that it was time to do what she wanted. It was really because of some spinal surgery she had and a battle with a cardiac problem.

"Her hair had turned completely white," Jensen says. "It was gorgeous, and she kept herself very pretty. She got to where she could slap those false eyelashes on with both eyes closed."

Jensen remembers the lashes once being the butt of a good "Harriet story": "We were at my house in Denver and Harriet was visiting. A couple of us girls had a little too much to drink, and I remember Harriet fell asleep on the couch in this beautiful green velvet dress.

"When I shook her to wake her up in the morning, she got up

and said, 'Have you got bugs?' and she started swatting with the pillow at this little black thing on the couch—it was her false eyelash!"

Harriet's own character could not have been more different from Mrs. Drysdale's. According to relatives, she was a "solid individual and very generous and giving."

In 1967 at Lenoir Rhyne College in Hickory, North Carolina, Harriet told students, "Don't criticize until you can equal or do better than that which you're criticizing. Have your opinions, but keep your mouth shut." And she discussed her reason for drifting out of theater and into television. "Why did I go into television work? Money!" she replied quickly. "Television work is safer and there's more security, and it pays better than theater. I find it very interesting. It is not personally or professionally as rewarding as the theater. You don't have the actor-audience contact. TV is very impersonal, but TV work is fun and I'm happy to be a part of the industry."

On February 8, 1987, Harriet succumbed to a massive heart attack after a cardiac ailment that affected the last years of her life.

ABOUT THE CREATOR . . . PAUL HENNING

Paul is a very fine writer. The thing that I
don't understand about Paul is why did
he stop writing? He had three big hits;
why the hell did he stop? He's a young fella.
Here I am at ninety-two—I work every day.
Paul, you ought to get a job!
—George Burns
April 1988

When Paul Henning was a Boy Scout back in Independence, Missouri, he spent his summers camping and hiking in the Ozark Mountains. On his treks through the hills, he met and became fascinated by real hillbillies.

"I've wanted to write something about these lovable people ever since," Henning said in a CBS biography.

Henning, born on September 16, 1911, was the youngest of eleven children. He worked his way through public schools by jerking sodas at a local drugstore. One of his customers, Harry Truman, advised Paul to go into politics. He might have taken Truman's advice if he hadn't gotten a job as a singer at KMBC Radio in Kansas City to finance his studies at the Kansas City School of Law.

Eventually, Henning learned that writing paid better than

PHOTO BY STEPHEN COX

Paul Henning in 1988.

singing on radio, or perhaps that his writing was better than his warbling.

In 1937, Henning sent his treatment for an episode of "The Fibber McGee and Molly Show" to Chicago; the script was bought, he was hired as a writer, and he moved to Chicago. After a year in the Windy City, he moved to California and worked as a freelance writer before starting regular stints on "The Rudy Vallee Show." He then joined the Burns and Allen show and spent the next ten years creating material for the couple's popular radio and television shows.

By this time, Henning had proposed by phone to his childhood sweetheart, Ruth Barth, in Kansas City, and they were married in Yuma, Arizona, on January 14, 1939. (Paul and Ruth will celebrate their golden anniversary in 1989—hillbilly style, no doubt.)

COURTESY OF PAUL HENNING

A young Paul Henning escorts
a contest winner from Kansas City. Here they
are visiting the Hal Roach Studio on the set of "Our Gang" with
little George "Spanky" McFarland, Darla Hood, and Billie "Buckwheat" Thomas.

In 1955, Henning created, wrote, and produced "The Bob Cummings Show" for CBS, a situation comedy about a Hollywood photographer with a roving eye for pretty girls. The show won several Emmys and was quite a success. He then collaborated with Stanley Shapiro on the story and screenplay of *Lover Come Back*, which gave him a nomination for an Academy Award in 1962.

The Hennings have three children, Tony, Carol, and Linda Kaye. Linda pursued an acting career and played the voice of Jethrine for "The Beverly Hillbillies," then later starred as Betty Jo Bradley on Paul's third successful television series, "Petticoat Junction," beginning in 1963.

COURTESY OF PAUL HENNING

Actors Bob Cummings and Charles Coburn
with Paul Henning on the set of ''The Bob Cummings Show.''

PHOTO BY STEVE COX

George Burns (sans his toupee)
gets together with family friends Ruth and Paul Henning in April, 1988.

Casts and crews assemble outside the mansion set to honor their producer, writer, and creator Paul as he enters the sound stage.

The comments of his associates indicate the esteem in which Paul is held. Al Simon says, "He is the best comedy writer around Hollywood or anywhere else. He accomplished things that no one else I know of in the business could accomplish. He's one of my best friends." Buddy Ebsen also calls him "one of my dearest friends. I love him," he says. According to Ted Switzer, "He made the show work. Truly a remarkable man." Bea Benaderet, quoted in *The New York Times*, said, "The true talent of the show is never seen." And Nancy Kulp says, "He's a genius in his field."

The list of compliments is endless. Henning deserves recognition not only as an unsurpassed talent, but as the gentle, kind friend he is to many, many people.

COURTESY OF VIACOM

Granny trades the open fire for the new-fangled stoves to do her cookin'.

GRANNY'S MENU

Top Twenty Vittles Prepared fer the Folks

- Catfish and apricot-gumbo soup
- Possum shanks (Cousin Pearl's favorite)
- Pickled hog jowls
- Gizzards smothered in gristle
- Smoked crawdads
- Grits 'n' black strap molasses
- Coot cobbler
- Homemade pickled pawpaws
- Sow belly 'n' hand-slung chitlins
- Fatback and black-eyed peas (et on New Year's Eve to bring good luck!)

- Possum-belly jam with a ham "omy-let"
- Dandelion greens
- Southern-fried muskrat
- Hog jowls melba
- Deviled hawk eggs
- Goat tripe
- Boiled mule
- Roast possum
- Stewed squirrel
- Ham hocks and turnip greens

Granny shore did love her cabin-cookin' and so did Jethro! Every time she'd throw together a mess o' greens, Jethro would have 'em et before dinner time!

Actually, the featured dishes above are real recipes that were mentioned on the show. At the height of the program's popularity, thousands of hill folk sent in recipes and suggestions for Granny to fix. Irene Ryan and writer Cathey Pinckney sorted all of the sug-

Jed and Granny discuss the finer points of butter churnin'.

COURTESY OF VIACOM

gested recipes and put together *Granny's Hillbilly Cookbook*, published by Prentice-Hall in 1966. Irene Ryan was so proud of the tome, newspapers reported she personally sent an autographed copy to President Lyndon B. Johnson at the White House. Lunch!

Here is one of the recipes from the list above. Granny loved to share her culinary secrets. Besides, "How else is a gal gonna hold on t' her man?"

DEVILED HAWK EGGS

Ozark Fixin's	Ingredients
a clod o' hard-cooked hawk eggs	12 hard-boiled eggs
a heap o' heated ham	1 cup cooked ham, diced
a tin o' milky toads	1 can, cream of mushroom soup
a heap o' thick milk, too	1 cup cream
a bit o' sweet spirits	½ cup sherry wine
a young onion	1 small onion, chopped
a quotom o' sweet pepper	1 small green pepper, chopped
a bit o' butter	2 tablespoons butter
a speck o' spicy salt	1 teaspoon seasoned salt

Fry up th' ham 'n sweet pepper 'n th' onion in th' butter 'til browned. Now dump in th' tin o' milky toads 'long with th' thick milk 'n sweet spirits 'n spicy salt. Keep yore heat mighty low 'n stir so it's all well-blended. Now toss in yore eggs and let 'em heat up easy like (5 minutes or so), makin' sure th' sauce never gits t' boilin'. Commence t' servin' in the fancy eatin' room.

Elly May cuddles with her critters on the set of the Hillbillies.

Elly's Critter Countdown

More than 500 animals were used on "The Beverly Hillbillies."
Everything from an ostrich to a skunk appeared as pets for Elly May.
Here, for the first time, are all of them there critters (or varmints,
Granny called 'em) that Elly befriended. Included are the cuddly
creatures and their names.

Bears: Johnny, Fairchild
Beetle: Cecil (Granny's weather-beetle)
Bobcat: Bobbie
Buzzard: Daisy

COURTESY OF FRANK INN

Hippo: "That was the show that almost killed us all," says director Joe Depew of the messy animal ordeal in the cement pond.

Cats: Rusty (swimming cat), Matilda
Chickens: Eleanor, Henrietta, Rosie, Drusilla, Florence, Viola, Jane, Lillie, Martha
Chimpanzees: Skipper, Bessie, Maybelle
Crow: Freddy
Deer: Maggie
Dogs: Arnie, Blue Chip (Mrs. Fenwick's unclipped poodle), Brutus, Gertrude, Hiram, Jo-Jo, Skippy, Wilbur, Ol' Duke (hound dog)
Duck: Gertrude
Eagle: Frieda
Fawn: Debbie
Goats: Clem, Thelma
Horses: Bessie (Pearl's), Silver-Trigger (Quirt Manley's), Lady-belle, Lightnin'

Kangaroo: Sidney
Kitten: Tommy
Lions: Jethro, Herman (mountain lion)
Mule: Nelson
Ostrich: Miriam
Owl: Henry
Pig: Porky
Pigeon: Florabelle
Poodles: Claude (Mrs. Drysdale's), Collette
Possums: Wendell, Mickey (albino possum)
Puppies: (Duke's) Cluade Fils, Claudette, Mimi, Jacques, Pierre
Racoons: Clyde, Davey Crockett, Elmer, Helen
Rooster: Earl
Seals: Whiskers, Raymond, Gloria
Skunks: Smelly, Charley
Squirrel: Mickey
Turkey: Herman

According to Donna Douglas, there is no mystery to her knack of working well with animals. The trick is to have a genuine love for them, she says.

"Animals—particularly those that are basically wild ones, such as raccoons, foxes, and cougars—can sense the actor who dislikes them or is afraid of them, and they react the same way," she says. "Even when the actor tries to mask his real attitude, the animals seem to be able to see through his disguise and detect the truth.

"I'm like Elly May in that I'm genuinely fond of all animals. I think even the most skittish ones sense this and therefore will at least tolerate handling by me. I've found that some of the most unlikely animals actually enjoy being cuddled and stroked if it's done by someone they sense strongly to be a friend."

Douglas remembers a scene in which Skipper, the chimp, was supposed to leap from her arms into the arms of an actor in the scene, and the chimp was to lovingly nestle there.

"This actor was a very nice guy, but as we were preparing to shoot the scene, he grumbled that he wasn't looking forward to being 'pawed by that crazy monkey' and that the sooner it was over, the happier he'd be."

Skipper responded, says Douglas, as if he had heard and understood what the actor had said.

"I practically had to throw Skip in order to transfer him to the man," Douglas says. Skipper refused to be held by him. Finally, director Joe Depew had to forsake the whole idea and get a rewrite of the scene.

COURTESY OF FRANK INN

Animal trainer Frank Inn and Donna Douglas pose with a samplin' of the critters: an owl, raccoon, and possum package.

Another important factor in working with animals, besides knack, is the trainer. And the Hillbillies had the best. His name was Frank Inn.

During the 1960s, Inn was kept mighty busy at General Service Studios catering to the animal needs of shows such as "The Bob Cummings Show," "Ozzie and Harriet," "The People's Choice," "Petticoat Junction," "Green Acres" (remember Arnold, the pig?) and of course nine years on "The Beverly Hillbillies." Since the seventies, Inn's familiar mutt, Benji, has remained one of America's most celebrated pets—and a movie star! But the Hillbillies show remains one of Inn's most rewarding—and tiresome—jobs.

The first animal chosen for the show was Inn's own hound dog, Stretch, which eventually became Ol' Duke. Then along came more than 499 other critters, all under the training and supervision of Inn, who worked wonderfully with animals. Only, the animals didn't always work wonderfully with Frank.

"This is about the funniest thing I remember about working on the show," Inn says. "The show had Elly May riding a hippo as it's swimming in the cement pond.

"The pond is only two feet deep and it took a full day to fill the pond with water. And after they got the water in, it took nearly another day to heat it well."

Inn explained that the hippo they were using was in love with an elephant and would not go anywhere without its beloved jungle giant. So to get the hippo into the pool, the elephant had to get in first and then step out and stay nearby dipping its trunk in the water so the hippo knew it was there.

"We practiced this routine to get control," Inn explains. "Donna was in her dressing room at this time. We led the elephant and the hippo in the warm water and as soon as they hit that water, they gave in to the wants of nature real quick!

"I mean, they both let it go and that water immediately turned the most putrid green that you had ever seen in your life! Elephant

COURTESY OF FRANK INN

Ol' Duke gets a bath for the next day's shooting. Duke's salary was $150 per episode, and he was treated like "royalty" by both the cast and the crew.

balls and all! And that stuff that came out of the hippo hit its tail like a fan. It was a mess."

Inn removed the animals while technicians skimmed the pool, but when the job was completed, the water was still green. So Inn suggested adding bluing to the water, as their time for shooting was quickly vanishing.

"It was the most beautiful pastel color," Inn says. "It was thick, but beautiful, like an artificial ocean."

"We got the hippo in the pool and it was OK. Then they asked Donna to come out and she remarked, 'Oh my, what a pretty blue. Why is the water so blue?' I said, 'Well, Donna, the reason is the hippo is supposed to be swimming and in the clear water you could see the bottom of the pool. She bought that!

"Next day at lunch, she gave me a heck of a whack across my shoulders. She knew then."

Joe Depew remembers how the animals, while usually tame and under Inn's control, sometimes showed their bad temper.

"We had a monkey that bit Irene one time," Depew, who detests working with monkeys, says. "It bit her on the arm hard. He hurt her badly and she screamed during the take, 'You son-of-a-bitch!' We had to take her to the emergency room to make sure she was all right.

"Monkees will be fine for years and years and suddenly turn on you," Depew adds. "They're messy, and I don't like them at all. Donna could handle them, though."

Of all her critters, Douglas says her favorite would be Skipper the chimp, who she used to swing between takes. "When Bessie, the second chimp, got big like Skipper we had to watch her," Douglas says. "Max [Baer] accidentally stepped on her foot and even when she got big, boy, she had her eye on him."

3
A CONVERSATION WITH MAX BAER, JR.

FEBRUARY 22, 1988

The question "Whatever happened to Max Baer?" still lingers today. Among the cast, Baer probably dodged reporters the most. He likes his privacy, as the large gates at the entrance of his home can verify. In this rare, exclusive interview, Max Baer shares some frank opinions regarding the series, his role as Jethro, and other factors relating to his big break in the entertainment business.

Q: *How easy was the role of Jethro for you?*

A: It came extremely easy to me. The lines weren't hard at all for me. It's one of those things. It's like some people can play basketball and some can play baseball. Some can hit. And others have to work hard at doing it. Everyone has an area that comes easier to them. I'm very poor in mathematics. Always have been. But philosophy and logic have been very easy for me. We're all different.

Q: *Max Baer is different from Jethro, isn't he?*

A: Oh yes. That's because you're hired as an actor, not as a person. They don't hire you because you are what you play. They hire you for whatever reason you seem to be able to do whatever they want or their image of what they want. That's it.

PHOTO BY GABI RONA

Hollywood photographer Gabi Rona captures
the two sides of Max Baer, Jr., in this special studio portrait.

Q: *What was the hardest part of the nine years on the show?*

A: Trying to keep the level up all the time. It's like the best marriage in the world—you still have bad days. You're still gonna fight. Parents fight with their kids and kids fight with the parents. Husbands and wives fight. Familiarity breeds contempt in many aspects. Buddy, Irene, Donna, myself, and the cast spent more hours per week with each other than we did with anyone we were married to or whatever. You better be able to get along pretty well; otherwise it's going to be a battle because you don't want to go to work on a daily basis with people you don't like.

Q: *Did the cast get along?*

A: Oh yeah. But first of all it's like a dog and a cat. They may be enemies, but if you put a dog and cat in a room together, they will learn to tolerate each other and get along because they know they have to do that to survive. I think that's the way most shows operate. It becomes very tedious for me to listen to all these people on the television shows tell how they're all a family and how they all love one another and are so happy together, when I know from experience that it's bull. They don't really get along. And they do have animosities. There are a lot of fights, but they aren't unusual. That's normal living. You may like or even love somebody, but from time to time, you're gonna get mad at them. I mean, I yelled at Irene and she yelled at me, I'd get mad at Donna and Donna would cry or something like that. Buddy would get angry with me and just turn his back on me.

But that's natural. Not everything runs smooth. It's obvious to anyone that has been fortunate to have a mother and a father that they fight and argue. Sometimes the closer you are the more you fight. But don't let anyone else pick on them—don't let anyone else yell at Donna, Irene, or Buddy. I can yell at them. But if somebody outside of our little clique said something, I'd tell them off.

On hiatus from the Hill-billies, Max Baer takes on a serious role in the movie *The Long Ride Home* in 1966 for Columbia Pictures. Baer wins critical acclaim as a well-honed versatile actor.

COURTESY OF COLUMBIA PICTURES

COURTESY OF VIACOM

Irene and Max share a laugh between scenes.

Q: *Was the whole cast protective of each other like that?*

A: Oh absolutely. You get that way. At first you don't know each other and it takes a while to get to know each other. There's certain things, then, that you don't like and certain things you do like. But you have to accept things you don't, just like a marriage. Just like your kid—you may not like a lot of things about your child but you accept it.

Q: *What about your own family—you're not married now, are you?*

A: No. I was married once. That was enough. I was divorced in 1971.

Q: *Was "The Beverly Hillbillies" lucrative for you?*

A: It was lucrative for my ex-wife. She got everything. Actually I didn't make that much. The first year of the series I made $500 a show. The second year of the series, I made $600 or $700 a show. The third year, we were the number one show in the country and I think I made $800 a show. The people who made the money were Filmways, the company who owned it, and Paul Henning, the writer, creator. Paul put in an awful lot of work on it and I'm sure he deserved the majority of it. However, I believe even in that time that, as a cast, we were not paid very well. There were fringe benefits. We could go out and earn extra money. But we didn't earn enough for what we did.

Q: *How well did you do on the personal appearance tours?*

A: We did reasonably well. Better than we did on the show.

Q: *Didn't your agent ask for more money?*

A: Yeah, but you see I was kind of a maverick, and I knew that in business you needed leverage. We all had different agents. Since Buddy was the star of the show going in, he got the most money. I think he got $2,000 a show, the first year. That's all. Donna and I got $500 each and Irene got $1,000. Ray Bailey might have got $1,000. I don't know what Nancy Kulp got. Maybe it was about the same with Donna and me.

So, I came up with an idea and said, "Hey, since Irene and Donna and I got along real well together and we went on the road together, we ought to get a mutual manager." So we got a manager named Eddie Sherman. He came with the suggestion that he

Max gleams at actress
Judy Jordan, who plays his
chauffeur when Jethro
is a big-time Hollywood agent.

COURTESY OF VIACOM

COURTESY OF VIACOM

"You'd be great in pictures, baby doll!" Jethro tries his hand at directing the voluptuous Gladys Flatt, played by semiregular Joi Lansing.

could go in and negotiate for the three of us together and make a better deal. The three together are leverage. I said "Terrific."

What happened is that when he went in to try to get more money for us, which we deserved—they were basically paying us damn near scale—and somebody told Paul that Irene would walk off the show if she didn't get paid. Paul really didn't like to get in the money end of it at all. He was basically the creative end of it.

But he got a call from Filmways that Irene, Max and Donna were gonna walk off the show. Paul Henning got crazy! He called up Irene and said, "Hey, why are you doing this to me? You didn't have anything before. . . ." And she didn't, which is true. He helped create a character which was terrifically advantageous to her. Irene got upset and she got hurt.

But business is business. If they could've had us work for nothing, they would've, and we're trying to get the moon. Therefore, Irene relented and told Eddie to negotiate for her individually. That broke the link. Once they got Irene, they went to Donna and the next thing you know, they were all dealing with individuals again. We never got what we should have gotten at all.

And I was made out to be the heavy because I suggested we go with Eddie so he could package us together.

I have no regrets. Everything's fair in business. Somebody's gonna win and somebody's gonna lose. We basically lost. *C'est la vie.* It's done.

Q: *Despite financial concerns, I heard you used to get extremely upset with yourself on the set sometimes when you delivered your lines wrong.*

A: I try very hard to be good at what I am doing. Imperfection bothers me. I get tremendously angry at my inability to do what I think I can do.

Another thing we used to say is that the script was the "bible according to St. Paul." That was Paul Henning. The producer/writer is up in his room, and you can't have people on the set changing lines and action and everything. If you do, you slow down the production. In a movie you can, but in TV you don't have the time and luxury. So therefore, to have everything run reasonably smooth as a business, Paul Henning had to have everything done his way and all the words his way. We were basically puppets. We'd do the lines exactly as they were.

If there was a question, we'd get on the phone and call Paul and ask and he'd say yea or nay. Most of the time, he would agree. Also, he'd then be aware of what's going on. It was effective. However, it was also extremely frustrating because sometimes we'd get into situations where we'd all get tongue-twisting lines we couldn't do.

Q: *That was a strict rule—not to change the lines—wasn't it?*

A: Yes. But I was probably the biggest violator of that rule. I guess it came from my natural gut feelings. I thought, if you wanted us to be puppets, you should have gotten dummies, stuff them or make them out of cloth and wood and have voice-overs.

Director Joe Depew rehearses a scene as Granny delivers a swift kick to Jethro's armor. Buddy is asleep standing up; Ebsen was known to be able to sleep at a moment's notice between scenes.

COURTESY OF JOE DEPEW

COURTESY OF FILMWAYS

Phil Gordon as Jasper "Jazzbo" Depew flirts with Jetherene Bodine.

Q: *Did you ad-lib a lot?*

A: No, but I'd change it into the way I would say it as Jethro. After you do it for a while, you become the character and the writer starts writing for you. In the beginning, you are doing what the writer has written. That happens on every successful television series. That's the way an excellent character is developed. Otherwise, you're never going to be able to grow any further than the original pilot screenplay. When you hire an actor, the actor's going to give you what you want plus some other things that you didn't even dream of.

Q: *Did you do this from the beginning?*

COURTESY OF VIACOM

"Listen t' yer maw!" Jed tells Jethro. Pearl is dressed in her fancy swimmin' outfit that ain't fit to get wet, but she does—when Granny shoves her in the cee-ment pond.

A: Pretty much so. But they didn't want me for "The Beverly Hillbillies." They wanted somebody else. They wanted somebody who's since passed away, a real nice guy and good friend of mine, Roger Torrey. They tested him, four times. He was big, the right size. He looked like a country bumpkin, and I was tested later in the afternoon. I didn't think I'd have a chance anyway, so I just laughed at everything. I bumped into things and laughed when I made the test with Buddy.

If I bumped into the doorjamb walking in, I'd say, "Excuse me!" and just laugh. Paul Henning told me later that when they saw it on the film, it was a dimension they had not thought about Jethro in. They expanded on that naïveté.

Q: *What did Paul Henning say to these additions to the script?*

A: He wasn't mad. Paul is a very bright man. And Paul is also up in a room, not down on the set. And sometimes things don't work. You can't write in a room and expect it to actually work because you may not have enough words to take you from point A to point B. They may be the wrong words for the action at the time. You don't have the time in television to be able to call the writer every five minutes when he's working on yet another script.

Q: *The show was Paul's baby, wasn't it?*

A: All the way. Paul's a good guy, too. Look, I can criticize Paul and at the same time thank him. If it wasn't for him I would've never had the job on probably the most successful television show of all time. At the same time, I can be critical because nobody's perfect and we all make mistakes and I make more than my share and I'm more than willing to admit it.

Q: *Years later when Paul approached you for the "return" movie, did you feel it wasn't good?*

A: No. I'm just too old to play Jethro. I'm a man, not a boy. I'm

Jethro is always flanked by women—once they find out his uncle is a millionaire!

COURTESY OF VIACOM

almost as old as Buddy Ebsen was when he played Jed. Personally I don't like digging up the dead bodies of old shows. I don't like to see the return of "Dobie Gillis," "Gilligan's Island," and a lot of different things.

Certain shows will lend themselves to growing up. We were almost like caricatures. We would not grow old gracefully because it's not charming for a forty-year-old man to play an idiot. It's not charming at forty. It's charming at eighteen.

To have Buddy come back, that's fine. If Irene were alive, to have her do it, that's fine. Agewise, they didn't change. We did. If they would have two new people instead of Donna and myself, maybe they would have something, and that was actually my suggestion. The premise bothered me. And I don't want to play Jethro for the rest of my life.

Q: *If the script had been much better, would you have done it?*

A: No. As a matter of fact, for the last seventeen years, I've only done about four parts as an actor. Reason being, that's what I wanted to do. I didn't want to do Jethro. I won't do guests on a weekly series. I did two shows, both for Michael Fisher, a friend of mine. I just don't have to. I made a lot of money in movies, with the ones that I own. So I don't have to work. I'm not going to do something I don't want to.

Q: *Did you watch the Hillbillies' reunion movie when it aired?*

A: No. I heard it was poor. It didn't have the charm. Granny wasn't there and, to me, Granny was the show. Buddy was a great straight man, a terrific actor, and a nice guy, but Irene was *it*. Without Abbott there wouldn't be any Costello. Without Costello, there wouldn't be anything. The comic makes it work. Irene was the foil. Irene and myself got the most, or were the brunt of the most jokes, not Buddy.

Q: *How did Irene feel about the success?*

A: Irene was just happy to be working. She worked hard for a lot of years and never really made it in this business, and when she got her shot, she was gonna ride that home into the sunset. She never wanted to make any waves.

That's why she didn't buck Paul Henning when the negotiations came down to money. She figured she'd have enough money to live on the rest of her life, which she did. She would rather not lose the job. She was so afraid of that and that was one thing that really bothered me. It was my first real understanding of somebody that was older. She'd been in the business forty years, had a chance to really do something, and the network and Filmways used leverage against her and scared her. She thought she'd never get another chance like this so she wasn't gonna risk losing it.

Q: *Did you like the job itself?*

A: Let's put it this way: I liked the first couple of years with Richard Whorf directing. After that, it became very mechanical. Joe Depew was Richard Whorf's assistant director. He was brought in after Whorf was fired to do exactly what Paul Henning wanted—make sure the lines were said, do the shots. Joe had never directed before. He was basically a sergeant at arms. I liked him; he was a nice guy. But Richard Whorf was an actor first. He was in *Yankee Doodle Dandy* and played Cagney's partner.

If I changed every line that [Paul Henning] wrote, he'd feel he had no worth. If I'd do every line that he wrote, I'd feel I had no worth. Now somewhere in between, there's a happy medium. And that was the constant battle. Buddy fought the battle. Irene fought it. Most of them would gripe, then let it go and do it. I was more reluctant. I'd go to the phone and call him and call him and call him. I'd call him more than anyone else and it became irritating to everybody, but that was the price they had to pay with me.

I knew I was dispensable. Nobody was indispensable on the show, except maybe Irene. But I had to do it.

I could have walked off [the show] and never done it again. I always had that choice.

Q: *Did you mind playing Jetherene?*

A: In one regard. I would go in and play Jethro in the morning. Take all the makeup off and put on a base which got rid of the beard that showed up in black and white. Play Jetherene. Then take the makeup off and play Jethro again. I'd do that two and three times a day. My skin was raw and all broken out. I said, "Hey, I'm not gonna do it." We switched the schedule and it worked better and the character was fun.

Any time you can play things other than yourself, it's fun. Many men playing women find it a tremendous release because it's a chance to use your imagination. I may not have done it well, but I was exercising my creative muscles, which makes it very satisfying to do.

Q: *How do you feel about Jethro now?*

A: Jethro's dead. It was something I was glad to do. I was proud to be a part of it. Probably more proud now than then in some respects. Some of my friends call me Jethro teasingly. It's like somebody calling you a son of a bitch. If he's your friend, it's OK. If he's your enemy, it's not. That's the way I feel about Jethro. It doesn't bother me like it did before. Sometimes I kind of enjoy it.

I'm not interested in living in the past or holding on to it.

Jethro takes the bull by the horns and
attempts yet another occupation—and
a dangerous one at that.

COURTESY OF VIACOM

Jethro in the Unemployment Line

Jethro never did find a job that satisfied his curiosity. Heck, he done graduated the sixth grade; what more could a sophisticated Hollywood playboy need? Herewith are the top ten careers that Jethro attempted. Remember these?

- Brain Surgeon
- Guru ("that name strikes a spark in my psyche.")
- Hollywood Agent/Director/Producer (C. B. deBodine)
- Protestor/Soul Brother/Flower Child
- Five-Star General
- Fry Cook (Jethro's restaurant: The Happy Gizzard)
- Atomic Scientist
- Psychiatrist
- Bullfighter
- Sophisticated Hollywood Playboy

4
"SO THEY LOADED UP THE TRUCK . . ."

For the season opening of the sixth year, Paul Henning was restless, so the idea of taking the show on the road was tossed around. What would be gained from such a trip, except extra cost? The list of advantages included that the series would be infused with new creative juices; it would mean a bright, new experience for the cast, all of whom had been with the series since its premier in 1962; it would mean an opportunity for new promotions and publicity to herald the coming of yet another new season; it would mean publicity in the area where they traveled, and it would mean an entirely new canvas of production settings that should delight the millions of viewers who continued to make the Hillbillies a top ten hit every year. All valid reasons.

The decision was made and budgets prepared. They were packin' their bags and skedaddlin'. Only they weren't just goin' yonder. They were going overseas to England.

This was the draft: Drysdale notifies Jed that he has inherited a Castle in Kent, England. Drysdale persuades the reluctant hillbillies to go to England to occupy it. His secret purpose is to accompany them to England, where he plans to become a big-time operator in English banking circles, but Jethro unintentionally complicates Drysdale's scheme. Dr. Granny also gets in the act, determined to cure whatever "decease" the marquess who bequeathed the castle to Jed is stricken with. The story

The cast poses in costumes for the England episode, filmed in London.

COURTESY OF FILMWAYS

featured a lavish array of Elizabethan costumes that Jethro thinks to be the proper English attire for visiting hillbillies.

The cast and key production personnel assembled in London in the early part of July 1967 and filmed from July 17 to July 21 at stately, majestic Penshurst Castle near Tonbridge, Kent. Filming was also done on the streets and at principal landmarks of the British capital.

The story just fit: the Clampetts' taste of foreign customs was a perfect vehicle for new gags to be introduced. Jethro had his outlandish knight's armor and a fit to fight the second War of the Roses between the Clampetts and the neighboring castle dwellers. Elly May was doin' her damsel in distressin' from the lofty tower. ("Donna was absolutely petrified up in that tower," says Nancy Kulp. "Who could blame her; it was scary.") Granny was temporarily thwarted from her doctorin' by a British customs inspector who confiscated her medical bag and its contents of wonder drugs: buckeye, snakewort, dogbane, horsemint, newt eyes, and cat hair.

Filming ran smoothly, and the international episodes were aired in succession at the beginning of the season. Not being on

COURTESY OF JOE DEPEW

Director Joe Depew points to the shot he wants at the Penhurst Castle in England. With him are writer Buddy Atkinson and Irene Ryan.

COURTESY OF FILMWAYS

William Tell he's not. Jethro aims for the fruit on their butler's head. The English servant Faversham (Richard Caldicott) takes care of the Clampetts at their castle in England.

COURTESY OF VIACOM

Granny in her Scottish kilt smells the roses from her garden outside the Clampett castle in England. She thinks the War of Roses is on between kin and the neighboring castle.

the soundstage did cause some distractions. Many details had to be carefully planned for the shooting, but production manager George King (who was "a genius at his field," according to Paul Henning), handled such details as transporting the truck and finding suitable grounds for filming. The truck was dismantled and shipped over piece by piece to save time—a precious commodity when filming on schedule. King scouted ahead for the castle, which he rented for the duration of the filming (the family owner, Lord De L'Isle, also ran tours through the manor to pay his taxes). The cast bedded in London's elegant Dorchester Hotel because the neighboring counties only had one inn with six rooms, which could not house the entire entourage.

"It was about an hour and a half to two hours' ride to location every day," says Joe Depew. "But Irene spent a few nights in the inn so she wouldn't have to worry about getting up so early to get to the location."

Every morning, the cast awoke while it was still dark and readied for the day's shooting. They passed each other in the lobby while grouping in taxis and limousines to be driven to the castle. Buddy Ebsen usually caught a little nap in the car while others would enjoy the beautiful English countryside or read through the day's script.

This drive was not the only inconvenience experienced in merry ol' England due to the visiting Hillbillies. "We were mobbed. We were shooting all over the city in costume and with the truck," Joe Depew remembers. "We were shooting in front of Buckingham Palace and not only were the tourists there to see the changing of the guard and all that jazz, but we had the English, too. My God, there were literally a thousand people around us. The cops, or bobbies they call 'em, were mad as hell. I often heard they are very polite, which they normally were. They used some of the King's English I'll tell you that. We had to get outta there."

The filming, although mobbed with fans and onlookers, ran on schedule and the storyline seemed well-received by the public as the new season of Hillbilly antics got underway. This venture was such a success, in fact, that for the seventh season in 1968, Henning and Al Simon decided to take the Hillbillies back to England to launch the second consecutive season opening in Europe. The key members of the production crew, cast, and writers assembled in London July 22 to begin filming four new episodes during their three-week stay. Again, the arrival was welcomed with a spot of tea and crumpets for our Hillbilly Brits.

HEADIN' FER HOME

The Beverly Hillbillies had been in residence in Californy long enough, Paul Henning decided. They were a heddin' back to the hills. Ozark, that is.

This billboard on Highway 44 in Missouri advertises the locally filmed episodes.

For the rhyme to fit the reason, Henning wrote a script-line that would force the Hillbillies back home: Granny hears the news that her nemesis, Elverna Bradshaw (Elvia Allman), has plans for her daughter's wedding. Granny bets Elverna she can get Elly a husband before the Bradshaw wedding takes place. So the Clampetts return home for the Silver Dollar City Fair with an ulterior motive—to find Elly a man.

In 1969, Henning took his show to the Missouri Ozarks to film on location. This marked a return to Henning's youthful days and memories of his first experiences that eventually led to the creation of the series.

Henning had made several trips to the Ozarks since he created the show, and many of the props, situations, and ideas for it came from Henning's observations. When the cast spent May 12 through May 17 filming at Silver Dollar City, a unique 2,000-acre development dedicated to the preservation of the arts and crafts of the Ozark hillpeople, it was a chance for the TV Hillbillies to meet the real folk from the hills.

No mention was made in the show that the Clampett family's home was in Missouri, however. The names of nearby cities, towns, and counties were spilled throughout the series' run, but a state was never revealed. Says Henning of this mandate: "We never identified the actual state location of the Clampett moun-

Fans mob the cast as they arrive in St. Louis in 1969. Irene and Donna make their way through the crowd after signing a few autographs.

COURTESY OF SILVER DOLLAR CITY

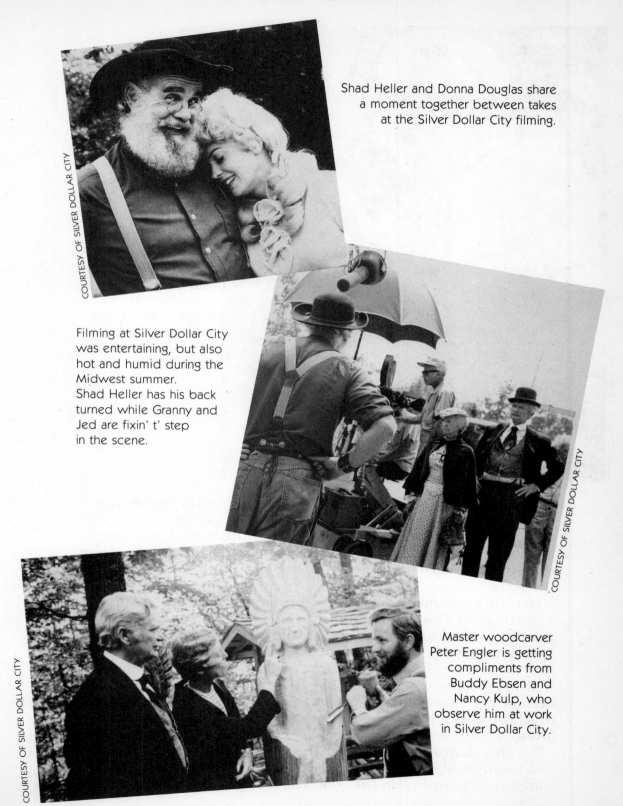

COURTESY OF SILVER DOLLAR CITY

Shad Heller and Donna Douglas share a moment together between takes at the Silver Dollar City filming.

Filming at Silver Dollar City was entertaining, but also hot and humid during the Midwest summer. Shad Heller has his back turned while Granny and Jed are fixin' t' step in the scene.

COURTESY OF SILVER DOLLAR CITY

Master woodcarver Peter Engler is getting compliments from Buddy Ebsen and Nancy Kulp, who observe him at work in Silver Dollar City.

COURTESY OF SILVER DOLLAR CITY

COURTESY OF SILVER DOLLAR CITY

Real life hillbilly Chick Allen attentively listens to one of Irene's show business squawks as they relax during the Ozark filming.

tain home. I feel just as strongly now as I did in the beginning of the show that it would be a mistake to limit the imagination of the viewer in any way. It's my belief that millions of loyal viewers believe that the Clampetts come direct from their own 'neck of the woods,' and that in some measure adds to their enjoyment of the show."

Henning also mentions that letters came from every state with a heritage of "hardy mountain people" indicating a feeling of great affection and kinship. He told the press while filming, "Heck, I grew up in Independence, Missouri, and I'd like to feel they come from the Missouri Ozarks. That's where I first saw the real hill people when I was boy. But the show has long since become the emotional property of the viewers and I don't intend to slight a single one of them. We'll be in the beautiful state of Missouri, but as far as the show goes, it'll be Anywhere, U.S.A."

For this Ozark trip, a special "task force" consisting of thirty-two highly trained persons—including the cast, of course—accompanied Henning on the trek. The group included: Harry Wolf

COURTESY OF SILVER DOLLAR CITY

A real Granny meets a reel Granny. Ethel Huffman, a lye soap maker at Silver Dollar City, talks with Irene during the filming in Missouri.

(head cameraman) and his crew of three, production manager George King, a script supervisor, a cost accountant, a sound engineer, a key grip, a dolly grip, a gaffer, a property master, a film editor, and two drivers. This put additional costs over regular studio production and neared $2,000 per person. A little project it was not, as more individuals accompanied them on the trip to Missouri than to England.

In addition, a group of Hollywood press correspondents accompanied the Beverly Hillbillies on their flight from Los Angeles. Other press and television reporters, photographers, and interviewers converged on Silver Dollar City from all over the Midwest to cover the production.

The Ozark episodes, directed by supervising film editor Bob Leeds in the absence of an ailing Joe Depew, drew viewers even from neighboring states to witness the filming. Hundreds of tourists watched the action and talked to the stars from behind police barricades.

The idea to film in the Ozarks originated in a letter to Paul Henning from Don Richardson, press and publicity agent for Silver Dollar City.

"I wrote Paul in 1965 and gave Paul an idea what this place was like," Richardson says of the Ozarks park. "Paul called me and told me that he'd like to visit the place sometime and I thought, yeah, yeah. Maybe sometime, only he's probably too busy. I didn't really think he'd do it. Then I got a call from Kansas City one day. It was Paul immediately wanting to visit and asking 'Where do I go from here?' "

Richardson helped make arrangements for the cast and crews in southern Missouri. They stayed at the Rock Lane Lodge while filming at the Silver Dollar City Hotel, the candle-making shop, the blacksmith shop, and the wood-carver's shop among other locations in the theme park. The inside set for the Silver Dollar City Hotel was replicated on the soundstage back in Hollywood where these scenes were shot.

Among the cast were some locals from the park—some were performers already—like Grannie Ethel Huffman, the lye soap maker, and master wood-carver Peter Engler. Performers such as fiddler Slim Wilson, who was made up to be a 100-year-old man in one scene, and Lloyd "Shad" Heller, an actor and blacksmith, were featured in roles.

Heller, who subsequently made appearances in four more episodes shot in Hollywood that season, also had a role in the reunion movie airing in 1981 on CBS.

NEW YORK, THE CAPITAL, AND MORE

Directly after filming in the Ozarks, the Hillbillies tangle with Phil Silvers for two episodes shot in and around Manhattan. Silvers played Shifty Schafer, better known as "Honest John," and of course, the Clampetts fall for his stories hook, line, and vittle. Shifty interests Jed in buying some "choice" pieces of Big Apple property, which he just so happens to have up for sale:

Central Park
SHIFTY: I'm willing to sell it to you as a sacrifice.
JED: It belongs to you, does it?
SHIFTY: Left to me by my late lamented Uncle—Sam Central.

Staten Island Ferry
JED: You own this boat?
SHIFTY: Picked up last month from my friend, Alexander Staten.

Brooklyn Bridge
SHIFTY: Have you ever thought of owning your own bridge?
JED: No sir.
SHIFTY: I have a bridge that I picked up at an auction last week from the estate of Oscar Brooklyn.

COURTESY OF FILMWAYS

Phil Silvers as Shifty, the role
he does best, in several episodes filmed in
Central Park in New York. (Watch where you put that hand, Max!)

As a hilarious surprise cameo appearance, the Hillbillies meet up with an Irish cop in Central Park, played by Sammy Davis, Jr., swinging his nightstick and spouting an accent that a leprechaun would be proud of.

The final travels for the Clampett clan came in their ninth and final season when they jetted to Washington, D.C., to help the President fight the national pollution problem.

The two Washington, D.C., episodes take the troupe to such sites as the White House grounds, the Lincoln Memorial, the Washington Monument, the Capitol, Dulles International Airport, Lafayette Park, the Smithsonian Institution's National

Zoological Park, the Pentagon, and the Supreme Court building.

In D.C., Jed and his family, concerned with the continuing menace of smog, take their money—now $95 million—to Washington and give it to the President to help solve the pollution problem. Drysdale, frantically trying to keep the Clampetts—and more importantly the anchor of his bank, otherwise known as the Clampett millions—at home, employs the services of special guest star Rich Little. Little, the master impressionist, impersonates President Nixon in an effort to convince the family that it won't be necessary for them to make the trip. He's a little *too* successful: the Hillbillies want to talk more with the President, pack their bags, and head for the nation's capital. Phil Silvers's role as con man "Honest John" recurs; he tries to intercept the Clampett fortune before it reaches the President.

At the conclusion of the filming schedule in Washington, the cast visited the Walter Reed Hospital in Washington and participated in the annual Spring Festival entertainment for more than 400 soldiers who had just returned from Vietnam. The program took place in the hospital's Red Cross Auditorium, with the Hillbillies being introduced by Major General Glenn J. Collins, Commander of the Walter Reed Army Medical Center.

Prior to the show-trips, in 1964, three of the cast members went on tour to capitalize on the extreme popularity of their characters. Irene Ryan, Donna Douglas, and Max Baer began a seventeen-day coast-to-coast personal appearance tour of eighteen cities on Friday, May 15, with a performance at the Cow Palace in San Francisco. They rehearsed and broke in an act during a pretour two-night stand in Tucson, Arizona, on May 9 and 10. Afterward, their schedule took them to Long Beach, California; Fort Wayne, Indiana; St. Louis; Dallas; Fort Worth; Houston; Pittsburgh; Chicago; Minneapolis; St. Paul; Sioux Falls, South Dakota; Des Moines; Charlotte, North Carolina; Baltimore; Philadelphia; Cleveland; and Milwaukee.

Also on the bill with the Hillbillies in this show were Spike Jones and Helen Grayco with the City Slickers, The Good Time Singers, the comedy act of Homer and Jethro, dancers calling themselves the Maldonados, Yonely the musical humorist, and the Rudenko Brothers, a troupe of jugglers.

After the tour, Irene Ryan joined Donald O'Connor in a four-week engagement beginning June 9 at the Sahara Hotel in Las Vegas to perform her single act, which won rave reviews on tour in the United States and the Tivoli circuit in Australia. During the acclaimed one-woman show, Irene performed what she called her "Granny Strip." She opened her show in costume as Granny and performed some bits and then abruptly stripped down to versatile actress and comedienne Irene Ryan, while a burlesque theme resounded throughout the nightclub.

Celebrities Join the Hillbillies

In the nine years that the Hillbillies resided in the hills of Beverly, where movie stars and socialites shine, Jed, Granny, and the gang played host to many of the biggest celebrities in town.

"We not only had guest stars on the show occasionally, but we had all the big ones stopping by the set to watch the filming or just say 'hi,'" says actor Phil Gordon, who played Jasper "Jazzbo" Depew early in the series. "Our set wasn't completely closed, so people like Lucille Ball, Phyllis Diller, members of the cast of 'The Addams Family,' Ricky Nelson, Minnie Pearl, and bunches of country and western stars loved to drop by."

Since this was the hottest show on television, actors were pleased—and even eager—to be cast for a guest shot or even a cameo appearance. Sharon Tate, who is more famous for her murder by the Charles Manson gang in the late sixties than for her acting, appeared in many episodes as Janet Trego, a member of the

COURTESY OF PAUL HENNING

The cast that never was. Actress Sharon Tate (left) was cast as the third daughter in the "Petticoat Junction" series. However, *Playboy* magazine published nude photos she had posed for prior to receiving the role. She was released from her contract for fear of scandal and negative publicity. With her are Bea Benaderet, Linda Kaye Henning, and Pat Woodall.

secretarial pool at the Commerce Bank. She always donned a black wig for the role.

"When we first got her she couldn't even walk through the door," says director Joe Depew of her lack of acting ability. "She was very amateurish. It was hard for her to read a line. Then she went to [acting] school and she learned a lot. She was a very pleasant girl and extremely beautiful . . . a real tragedy."

Max Baer dated Tate during the series and comments: "She was a lovely girl, but I never got that close to her."

"The Beverly Hillbillies" also played host to many classic stars and actors who are recognized worldwide for their talent, and the show let them demonstrate it. The whopping list of stars who made guest appearances on The Beverly Hillbillies includes:

- Eddie Albert
- Lola Albright
- Jim Backus
- Mel Blanc
- Pat Boone
- Foster Brooks
- Edgar Buchanan
- Sebastian Cabot
- John Carradine
- Ted Cassidy
- Roy Clark
- Hans Conired
- Wally Cox
- Bob Cummings
- Sammy Davis, Jr.
- Richard Deacon
- Rosemary DeCamp
- Leo Durocher
- Eva Gabor
- Henry Gibson
- Hedda Hopper
- Bernie Kopell
- Rich Little
- June Lockhart
- Paul Lynde
- Meredith MacRae
- Ralph Morgan
- Julie Newmar
- Rob Reiner
- Don Rickles
- Hayden Rorke
- Charlie Ruggles
- Soupy Sales
- Natalie Schafer
- Phil Silvers
- Gloria Swanson
- Sharon Tate
- Arthur Treacher
- John Wayne
- Jesse White
- Mary Wickes
- Paul Winchell

Of all the celebrities visiting the Clampett domain, the most memorable to the cast was probably John Wayne, who made a cameo appearance in an episode titled, "The Indians Are Coming."

"We wrote that bit in for him because Buddy was a good friend of Duke's and called him," Paul Henning says. "He said he liked the show and would be glad to do it. It was such a quick little bit, I don't even think they bothered with makeup for him."

COURTESY OF JOE DEPEW

John Wayne surprises Irene, "his biggest fan," when he ambles on the set to make a cameo appearance in the episode "The Indians Are Coming." Wayne was a fan of the show and eager to appear with Granny.

Nancy Kulp remembers one of her favorite guest stars with fondness. It was the endearing star of TV's "Mr. Peepers," Wally Cox, who played Professor Biddle, a gentle bird-watcher—not unlike Cox's true persona. Kulp reverted to her old character as a bird-watcher (similar to Pamela Livingstone, on "The Bob Cummings Show") to play almost exclusively opposite Cox in two episodes of the Hillbillies.

"He was a very gentle, very soft-spoken man. I knew him well," Kulp says. "It was hard not to like Wally. Everyone was fond of him. One year, he came to my house for Thanksgiving on a motorcycle with his daughter behind him."

For the most unique of all guest shots, the award would have to go to the late Gloria Swanson, star of the silent screen. She was pulled out of retirement to star in the classic movie *Sunset Boulevard* (1950), but television appearances were a rarity. She did "The Beverly Hillbillies," however.

In this hilarious and nostalgic episode, the Hillbillies catch Gloria

COURTESY OF VIACOM

Silent film star Gloria Swanson comes out of retirement to appear as herself on "The Beverly Hillbillies." Jed, thinking she is destitute, gives her a role in an ol' fashion movin' picture he produces and stars in.

WRITE IT—DON'T SAY IT INTER-DEPARTMENT MEMORANDUM

TO PAUL HENNING   BETTY BOND   DATE OCT. 3 19 66   A.M.
   AL SIMON   RON BECKMAN   P.M.
   JOHN NICOLAIDES   TOM KELLY
   TED LANGWELL   HARRY HOGAN
   GEORGE KING   #5000-150

SUPPORTING CAST MEMBERS OF "THE GLORIA SWANSON" EPISODE
OF THE BEVERLY HILLBILLIES ARE:

   GLORIA SWANSON (HERSELF).....................$2500 FOR WK.
       (SEP. CARD SPECIAL GUEST STAR BILLING)
   MILTON FROME (LARRY CHAPMAN)................. $725 FOR 2
       (AFTER NANCY KULP- "AND MILTON AS LARRY CHAPMAN")
   GEORGE NEISE (AUCTIONEER)....................$500 FOR 2
   LENNIE BREMEN (MOVER 1)......................$150 FOR 1
   FRANK SULLY (MOVER 2)........................$150 FOR 1
   LENORE KINGSTON (WOMAN)......................$150 FOR 1
   DANIEL WHITE (MAN)...........................$150 FOR 1
   RAY KELLOGG (STUDIO GUARD)...................$200 FOR 1

                                          Bill
REPLY ON THIS SHEET   FROM   BILL TINSMAN

WILMER "SERVICE LINE"   STANDARD INTER DEPT MEMO. FORM 11-24

COURTESY OF PAUL HENNING

Gloria Swanson was possibly the highest paid guest star on the show. Here, a payroll memo shows her receiving a hefty $2,500 for the week. For today's standards, it's peanuts.

in her home preparing to move. Many of her items are boxed and being hauled out of her house, leaving Jed to think she's poor and her belongings are being taken. Jed decides to star her in a movie for the studio he owns, and an updated "silent" film was born—or reborn.

"Gloria Swanson was nice to work with, a thorough pro," says Paul Henning, whose idea it was to invite her on the show.

"Everyone was very much in awe," remembers Nancy Kulp of Swanson's appearance. "Most of the time, she worked with me. I remember on the set she kept telling me not to eat white sugar. She lived to a ripe old age and she had a very stringent diet; everything had to be natural. She said that white sugar was poisoning the world. I don't want to ridicule her, though, that was her thing. In fact, I don't eat much white sugar."

COURTESY OF VIACOM

Soupy Sales as Lance Bradford, Mrs. Drysdale's nephew, arrives home from the Air Force and interests Jethro in the service.

Gentleman's gentleman Arthur Treacher guest stars.

COURTESY OF VIACOM

5
THE
BEVERLY HILLS
BOMB

ENDING THE ERA

The rural situation comedies of the sixties that struck oil for networks, like the Hillbillies, were all axed off the schedule in one swift swing. For the 1971 season, the roster would not include "The Beverly Hillbillies," "Green Acres," "Mayberry R.F.D.," "Hee Haw," or "The Don Knotts Show."

In the early sixties, the Hillbillies were the vanguard of the second "cluster" of rural comedies. Paving the way for the Clampetts were "The Egg and I" (1951–52), "The Real McCoys" (1957–63), and "The Andy Griffith Show" (1960–68). The Hillbillies also fathered "Petticoat Junction" (1963–70) and "Green Acres" (1969–71).

It seems that upper brass at CBS wanted to trade its countrified programming for a more sophisticated genre of selections. The loyal viewers who had watched rural-oriented shows throughout the decade were disappointed after the cancellations. So were the casts. Irene Ryan, especially, was madder than a wet hen, a hillbilly might say, over the programming cuts. But life went on and the Hillbillies left the air . . . for a while.

In the latter seventies and early eighties, rural programming made a comeback with "The Dukes of Hazzard" and "Sheriff Lobo." Although not as funny as the sitcoms of the sixties, the programs received moderate-to-good ratings.

So the idea was proposed that the Clampetts should return . . . and they did. Unfortunately.

111

Y'ALL COME BACK NOW

Actually, this bomb occurred back home in the hills for the Hill-billies.

Granny had gone to her reward. Jed had divided up his fortune among Jethro and Elly May and they had invested in their re-spective interests: Jethro was the owner and head producer of Mammoth Motion Picture Studios, while Elly May was the owner of her own zoo. Mr. Drysdale had gone to the great mint in the sky while Miss Hathaway—still *Miss* Jane—now was a Washing-ton, D.C., "career girl" working for the government. Jed sold his Beverly Hills mansion and moved back to the cabin where it all started—only he added on to the cabin to provide a little more space.

COURTESY OF PAUL HENNING

Miss Jane gets her man—almost: Werner Klemperer and Nancy Kulp star in "The Return of the Beverly Hillbillies."

This was the opening sequence of the made-for-television movie in 1981, *The Return of the Beverly Hillbillies*, which picked up where the series left off. Creator Paul Henning had reassembled part of the cast: Buddy Ebsen, Nancy Kulp, and Donna Douglas. Max Baer did not wish to return to the show that boosted him to fame, so Jed, Elly May, and Miss Jane were the only remnants of the original show. The return lost more than characters; it lost the original humor that made the show so popular.

Henning did, however, write the show, while previous film editor and occasional director Bob Leeds (now in the process of a divorce from Donna Douglas) joined in for the last hurrah. Actors Shad Heller and Shug Fisher, who appeared in several episodes in the sixties, also had roles in the two-hour prime-time special. Earl Scruggs flew in from Tennessee to contribute some guitar picking, but his old bluegrass partner of many years, Lester Flatt, had since died.

One can only hope that this was the last of its kind, as the movie bombed in the ratings, as well as turning out to be a scrap heap for fans to remember their ol' Hillbillies by.

Factors contributing to the production's failure were many. For Donna Douglas, it was the movie's lack of nostalgia: "If you think about it, it had none of the original premise. No roots. The house was gone, the car was gone. No bank. Drysdale was not there, and the only cast members from the original were me, Buddy, and Nancy. The anchors were just not there."

There were more reasons than nostalgia to bring back the Hillbillies. As Paul Henning explains, it was mainly financial, which proved unlucrative anyway. Rebuilding the original sets proved costly and was quickly squelched, so Henning wrote the movie around Jed's cabin in the back hills.

"It was purely a business enterprise. Purely a chance to make some money," Henning says. "A fellow by the name of Ron Beckman, who had been in charge of contracts at the old studio, came to see me and said he thought we could reap a financial harvest by having the Hillbillies get together again.

But Henning was not in the best of health at the time and was on medication that affected his creativity.

"I had started taking a blood pressure depressant to hold down my blood pressure, which was dangerously high," Henning explains. "I didn't want to have a stroke. I took medicine, and it did indeed lower the blood pressure, but it also lowered my awareness. I called it a pharmaceutical lobotomy."

To complicate matters, Henning sat down with the cast and read-throughs proved the script not up to the old Hillbilly standards—or any humorous standards. Simultaneously the Writers Guild went on strike, and Henning could not alter the script.

Jed, a little older and possibly a little wiser, proudly observes Miss Jane's wedding.

COURTESY OF VIACOM

Henning did not have the time or the capacity to rewrite the script, so the story remained much the same, to the disappointment of those involved—especially Henning, one of television's most talented writers.

"I take full responsibility for the failure of *The Return of the Beverly Hillbillies*," says Henning. "It was a bad script and I knew it was a bad script and when it came time to rewrite it, the Writers Guild went on strike. I was helpless, 'Between a rock and a hard place,' as a hillbilly would say."

Once again, Buddy Ebsen applied his fake mustache and dusted off the torn hat and tan jacket to spout a "Well Doggies" for the fans. Donna Douglas fit right back into rope-tied jeans to hug the critters. The cast also included Imogene Coca as Granny's 104-year-old Maw. Werner Klemperer, who starred in TV's "Hogan's Heroes" as the inept German Colonel Klink, starred as C. D. Medford, a government bureaucrat who almost marries Jane Hathaway. Actor Ray Young, who looked similar to Max Baer, filled in for the role of Jethro, and Linda Kaye Henning played the role of Jethro Bodine's secretary at the motion picture studio.

White-bearded Shad Heller from the Silver Dollar City episodes flew in once again from the Missouri Ozarks with his wife Molly, also an actress, to reprise his role as Jed's hillbilly buddy.

"We missed Granny terribly," Heller says of the reunion movie. "And Max was a loss, too. He said yes originally to Paul when he was approached about the part. He kept saying yes, but when it got close to filming, Paul could not get hold of Max. He was dodging Paul. Finally Paul sent someone to see Max, and Max refused the part at the last minute, so they found this other guy who looked a little like Jethro, but wasn't a seasoned actor. He did what he could."

Baer later explained:

"I was twenty-five years older." "I don't think it would have worked for me." Baer tried to shy away from his identification with the role that most viewers of the show, and unfortunately, most casting directors perceived. "I felt trapped in that part from the beginning. I felt that way when I first did it. Just like Archie Bunker. Carroll O'Connor will always be Archie Bunker."

COURTESY OF PAUL HENNING

Ray Young takes the place of Max Baer as Jethro Bodine in "The Return of the Beverly Hillbillies." No one could play the part the way Baer did, nor should anyone have tried.

Baer was not the only original cast member to feel the difference. "It wasn't the same," Nancy Kulp says. "It was very difficult. I never thought Imogene Coca was good casting, but [the producers] did and I wasn't going to say anything. Director Bob Leeds used these idiotic shots, many over-the-shoulder shots that don't lend themselves to comedy. It was atrocious. But I must say it was good to get back together with some of the people from the show."

The plot was simple—unlike some of the early vintage Hillbilly episodes which sometimes contained a network of subplots all moving toward one hilarious upshot.

Comedienne Imogene Coca stars as Granny's 104-year-old Maw, the only living soul with the secret recipe for Granny's "white lightnin'."

COURTESY OF PAUL HENNING

Miss Hathaway and her associate, C. D. Medford, fly from Washington on special assignment from the president to get a sampling of Granny's white lightin', which she brewed in her still. This potent concoction was believed by Miss Hathaway to be the way to eradicate the energy crisis for good.

Upon her return to the hills, she is reunited with the Clampett patriarch—and to several empty jugs of white lightnin'. The only living soul who knows the recipe is Granny's 104-year-old Maw who whips up a batch only for special occasions. So Miss Jane and her associate, Medford, reluctantly marry and a wingding takes place at the Clampett's once again.

It ends up that Jed knew the marriage was not made for love and he arranged for a substitute judge, so the marriage was never valid. And the white lightnin' was accidently consumed by Medford.

The film was well-publicized with promos airing regularly. Articles were being run in almost every major newspaper including interviews with the cast. Hopes for a resurgence in popularity and a new series were being dangled in front of viewers' eyes by the press. But was creator Paul Henning ready for another series? "No, frankly," he says. "I didn't want to get back into that glass furnace." Henning also reluctantly admits the film did not reap the harvest intended. The corn was planted too late, some think.

The movie did not fare well in the ratings that October 6, 1981, on the season premiere of the CBS "Tuesday Night Movies." This was the evening that every network interrupted their broadcasts to relay the news that Egyptian President Anwar Sadat had been assassinated. A ratings booster this was not; however, the scores would have put them in third place (among the three networks) regardless. Even a rebroadcast on the CBS "Saturday Night Movie" on July 7, 1984, brought less-than-favorable ratings. Movie and television historian Leonard Maltin noted that taking the Hillbillies out of "comfortable retirement in TV heaven" was not a wise choice and rates the film "below average."

Faithful watchers of the Hillbillies winced at the reunion yet knew it was nice to set a spell with their friends once again. The hillbillies always said, "Y'all come back now, y'hear?" . . . and they did—only the viewers didn't.

COURTESY OF PAUL HENNING

Paul Henning stands tall in his success with the two stars of his show, Buddy Ebsen and Max Baer.

6
LAUGHING ALL THE WAY TO THE COMMERCE BANK

Valid social criticism with a top-ten Nielsen
is an absolute rarity in television. This
is the true measure of the success of
"Beverly Hillbillies"—the first of its kind.
Saturday Review
January 5, 1963

Despite long, successful runs of Paul Henning's creations, plus a good mark for his collaboration on TV's "Green Acres," he was never recognized by his peers.

Truly recognized, that is. The show was recognized with a few nominations but never rewarded with an Emmy. The Academy of Television Arts and Sciences nominated Henning for Emmys for Outstanding Program Achievement in the Field of Humor and Outstanding Writing Achievement in Comedy in 1962–63. Henning lost out to "The Dick Van Dyke Show" and Carl Reiner, respectively. During the second season (1963–64) of the Hillbillies, after the show had reached number one in the nation, Irene Ryan was nominated for Outstanding Continued Performance by an Actress in a Series but lost to Shirley Booth who starred in the NBC Series "Hazel," and in 1967 Nancy Kulp lost the award for best supporting actress. Director Richard Whorf was also nominated but did not win.

Remembers Al Simon: "We all attended the Academy presentation that second year of the show. We didn't win anything, but I will tell you this . . . after Dick Van Dyke went up and received his Emmy, honest to God, he looked over to our table where Paul was sitting and bowed."

The assumption was that "The Dick Van Dyke Show," whose ratings were not impressive upon its airing, was pulled up from the depths after being scheduled directly following the Hillbillies

COURTESY OF PAUL HENNING

Production supervisor George King, revered by his cohorts, receives this honor on the set, much to his surprise.

COURTESY OF SILVER DOLLAR CITY

The cast assembles to give the Distinguished Native Son award to Paul Henning.

COURTESY OF FILMWAYS

The progress of American astronaut Leroy Gordon Cooper was flashed on the screen during the prime time airing of the Hillbillies. This debut mission of Cooper's took him around the earth twenty-two times on NASA's thirty-four-hour Faith 7 flight.

on Wednesday nights. "The Dick Van Dyke Show," riding on the Clampetts' coattails, was raised from number nine in the ratings its first year to number three after the Hillbillies went gold.

After that first fateful Emmy night of May 26, 1963, when the Hillbillies went home empty-handed, Carl Reiner, creator of "The Dick Van Dyke Show," sent a letter to Paul Henning thanking him for his congratulations; Reiner also gave his sincere regrets that the Hillbillies did not win an Emmy, although they were much more popular than Reiner's show. Moreover, Danny Thomas, the Van Dyke show's top man and also a Hillbilly fan, sent Henning a box of cigars.

"The year that we were nominated," says Nancy Kulp, "the Hillbillies were invited to present something, but they wanted them in costume. It was very demeaning. Since then, I've walked out on the Academy.

"By the time I was nominated for an Emmy in '67, none of us were members of the Academy at all and I've never gone back. I'm a member of the Screen Actors Guild, however, and the Motion Picture Academy."

This loss at the Emmy Awards was not the first crushing blow

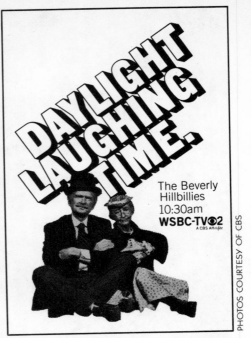

The show was so popular in prime time that CBS placed the program in its daytime schedule, where it did well.

to the Hillbillies. Irony surrounded the series' whole existence: the ratings were overwhelming, yet the recognition for the creator and performers by peers was near zero. While viewers loved the show, the critics initially abhorred the corn-fed humor. This sharp criticism hurt, yet only served to give more publicity to the show.

"The thing that angered and infuriated us most was the lack of recognition they gave Paul for his brilliance," said Nancy Kulp. "I think the man is a genius. And these half-baked entrepreneurs in Hollywood didn't seem to recognize that humor doesn't necessarily speak in an English accent. It was the pseudointellectuals that tried to tear us apart.

"At first we were very angry, then we just got used to it and kept hoping time after time that Paul would get an award."

But the true award lies in the inclusion of the Hillbillies in the list of top-rated programs of all time. According to the A. C. Nielsen ratings system, "The Beverly Hillbillies" has the honorable distinction of claiming an incredible eight appearances for individual episodes on the list of the top twenty shows. These episodes share the list with such television phenomena as the final episode of "M*A*S*H" and "Dallas's" "Who Shot J.R.?" episode.

The top-rated individual episodes of all time are as follows:

Show	Network	Date	Rating
1. "M*A*S*H" (finale)	CBS	2/28/83	60.2
2. "Dallas" ("Who Shot J.R.?")	CBS	11/21/80	53.3
3. "The Fugitive" (the famous final episode of the series)	ABC	8/29/64	45.9
4. "Ed Sullivan Show"	CBS	2/9/64	44.6
5. "Beverly Hillbillies"	CBS	1/8/64	44.0
6. "Ed Sullivan Show"	CBS	2/16/64	43.2
7. "Beverly Hillbillies"	CBS	1/15/64	42.8
8. "Beverly Hillbillies"	CBS	2/26/64	42.4
9. "Beverly Hillbillies"	CBS	3/25/64	42.2
10. "Beverly Hillbillies"	CBS	2/5/64	42.0
11. "Beverly Hillbillies"	CBS	1/29/64	41.9
12. "Beverly Hillbillies"	CBS	1/1/64	41.8
13. "Bonanza"	NBC	3/8/64	41.6
14. "Beverly Hillbillies"	CBS	1/22/64	41.5
15. "Bonanza"	NBC	2/16/64	41.4
16. "Bonanza"	NBC	2/9/64	41.0
17. "Gunsmoke"	CBS	2/28/61	40.9
18. "Bonanza"	NBC	3/28/65	40.8
19. "Bonanza"	NBC	3/7/65	40.7
"All in the Family"	CBS	1/8/72	40.7 (tie)

PHOTO BY DAWN ERICKSON, COURTESY OF RALPH FOSTER MUSEUM

The wheels have stopped turning for the Hillbilly-mobile, recognized around the world. Paul Henning donated the classic vehicle to the Ralph Foster Museum at the School of the Ozarks in Branson, Missouri. The 1921 Oldsmobile four-cylinder "didn't handle at all," says Max Baer, who always drove the flatbed. "It could hardly take corners and it was sometimes hard to shift."

Notice, the highest rated of these aired on January 8, 1964. This episode of the Hillbillies, titled "The Giant Jackrabbit," has remained the highest rated half-hour episode of any television show since 1960. The month of January 1964, The Hillbillies rode high on the hog, as every episode ranked in the top eleven. Weekly rating shares were kind, and the show did unbelievably well during the whole nine-year span.

The ratings history of "The Beverly Hillbillies," out of the top twenty-five shows each year, is as follows:

Year	Rank	Rating
1962–63:	#1	36.0
1963–64:	#1	39.1
1964–65:	#12	25.6
1965–66:	#8	25.9
1966–67:	#9	23.4
1967–68:	#12	23.3
1968–69:	#10	23.5
1969–70:	#18	21.7

COURTESY OF PAUL HENNING

A collage of Hillbilly art illustrates how widespread their popularity was. *TV Guide* used them on the cover seven times—three in one year. Circulation went up each time they appeared.

The Radio and Television Women of Southern California honors actress Bea Benaderet at its twelfth annual Genii Award Banquet April 15, 1966. Paul Henning and Buddy Ebsen were present to help congratulate.

COURTESY OF KATHY HUDSON

"The Beverly Hillbillies" has surpassed every show in the history of the rating system with its eight top-rated episodes. It is safe to say that no show ever made it to the top so quickly. By the second two-week national Nielsen Television Index report, "The Beverly Hillbillies" was the top-rated show in the nation. Essentially, it remained on top the first two seasons it was on the air.

The argument has been raised—especially by entertainers who didn't fare well in the ratings—that the Nielsen race is nothing short of television politics. Can the ratings be trusted, and are they an accurate reflection of the viewers' taste?

In 1963, *TV Guide* magazine took a readers' poll, more aptly referred to as the Viewers Poll, and asked what the people really thought. Once again, the Hillbillies conquered the public. They were acclaimed the best new show of the year by more than a quarter-million *TV Guide* readers.

Since television has been called "America's vast wasteland," one writer retorted, "The Hillbillies must be Death Valley." Ap-

Donna Douglas got a tour of the Sanyo plant in Gumma Prefecture, outside of Tokyo. There she met Sanyo officials and employees, attended an "autograph party," and was the guest of honor at a reception given by *Hi Lady*, a Japanese women's magazine.

COURTESY OF GEORGE FABER

praisal such as this was not appreciated, of course. "You've got to feel bad," Paul Henning told a reporter in 1964, at the height of the harsh criticism. "After all, I'm human." Henning also said many intellectuals had written and congratulated him on the show, although they could not muster the courage to watch the show with the blinds up or the curtains open.

The program was not only a favorite in America and Australia, where it won an award for best overseas program; the show was also a hit in the United Kingdom.

When, in 1963, "The Beverly Hillbillies" was first offered to broadcasters on the British Isles, no network was interested, remarking that none of their viewers would understand the comedy of Ozark hillbillies. One of the United Kingdom's fourteen regional broadcasters, however, had a different opinion. That was Granada TV, Ltd, which began broadcasting the series in northern England in February 1963.

Granada's enormous success with the show soon attracted the attention of other regional broadcasters, and in 1964, it was being transmitted in eleven of the fourteen regions into which the United Kingdom is divided.

According to a 1964 study of the British television audience prepared by TAM (Television Audience Measurement, Ltd.), a British company, "The Beverly Hillbillies" was being seen in more than six million of the thirteen million television homes in Great Britain, with ratings ranging from the upper thirties to the lower fifties with a high of sixty in southern England.

Another country to honor the show with enormous popularity was Japan. The Nihon Television Network, Corporation (NTV), which broadcasted "The Beverly Hillbillies," and the Sanyo Electric Manufacturing Company, which sponsored it, acted on this rage and invited Donna Douglas to make an eleven-day personal appearance tour (starting May 17, 1963). Douglas spent a week in Tokyo and was a featured guest performer on two NTV musical variety programs, "Shabondama Holiday," and "Seventeen." The Japanese crowds proved to be the same as those in the United States and Australia—swarming. Rickshaws and Toyotas zeroed in on every locale where Douglas was appearing, in hopes that fans could get a look at the honorable Elly May "Crampott"-san.

AWARDS, THAT IS!
HONORS, RECOGNITION, POPULARITY . . .

- Irene Ryan was honored as Woman of the Year by the National Father's Day Committee at the annual Father of the Year Awards Luncheon held at the Waldorf-Astoria Hotel in New York. The citation noted, "Besides being active in the entertainment world, Miss Ryan has taken an active part in charity causes, aiding such campaigns as the March of Dimes, American Heart Association, Community Chest, and Medicare Alert and performing for veterans in hospitals across the country."

- At a press reception concluding a week of filming "The Beverly Hillbillies" in Washington, D.C., a certificate of appreciation from the United States Coast Guard was given to Buddy Ebsen for "notable services" in the production of a series of television films on proper boating. Ebsen, a yachtsman of national prominence and winner of several major boating competitions, served with the Coast Guard in World War II. Rear Admiral J. J. McClelland presented the award in the studios of WTOP-TV, a CBS affiliate in Washington, D.C.

- "The Beverly Hillbillies" won Australia's most coveted television honor, the "Logie Award," as the most popular overseas program series broadcast in Australia. Donna Douglas accepted the invitation to visit Melbourne, Australia, to receive the golden statuette on behalf of the cast. The presentation

COURTESY OF *TV WEEK*

Australia's Logie awards presented "The Beverly Hillbillies" with the award for the most popular overseas program series broadcast in Australia. Donna Douglas accepted the award at Melbourne's Palais de Dance. Here she is shown with Australian Gold Logie winner Jimmy Hannan.

took place during a charity ball on Friday, March 26, 1965, sponsored by *TV Week* magazine, which conducted the poll to determine its winners. In attendance were much of Australia's officialdom, including the State Premier and Melbourne's Lord Mayor.

- Irene Ryan, who observed her fiftieth year in show business in 1967, was honored with the Genii Award by the Radio and Television Women of Southern California at the thirteenth annual Genii Award banquet at the Beverly Hilton Hotel in Beverly Hills, California, on Saturday, April 15, 1967.
- The "Show Me" state of Missouri showed Paul Henning what it thought of him with a special "Distinguished Native Son" award created for him by then-Governor Warren E. Hearnes. The presentation was made by Mrs. Hearnes in May of 1969 when Henning took his Hillbillies to the Missouri Ozarks to

film parts of five episodes to be shown throughout the year's season.

- During her Hawaiian vacation, notes a 1967 CBS press release, Irene Ryan was crowned "Queen of Kauai," an honor that was the realization of a lifelong ambition for the wispy little actress. "I always wanted to be the Queen of something—anything," said Ryan, "but with a figure that reads twenty-one from top to bottom, I never felt I had a chance against the usual 36–23–36 competition. Then, suddenly, it happened, and there I was, a Queen at last!"

- October 20, 1965, was officially proclaimed as Possum Day in Beverly Hills, California. Mayor Frank Clapp saluted the cast of the Hillbillies on the steps of the Beverly Hills City Hall with all of the main members present to lead the festive tribute to the homely marsupial. The entree at the luncheon, by the way, was possum.

- The American Humane Society honored Donna Douglas with a special award, and stars of both "The Beverly Hillbillies" and "Petticoat Junction" were cited at the annual convention of the Los Angeles metropolitan district of the California Federation of Women's Clubs. Douglas was cited for "consistently demonstrating kindness and compassion for a wide assortment of living 'critters' and making a valuable contribution to the humane cause." She received the honor at the fourteenth annual "Patsy" award ceremonies of the American Humane Association at the RKO Pantages Theater in Hollywood.

Hillbillies on Parade

In the heyday of the show, marketing executives for CBS decided that Hillbilly merchandise was a worthwhile investment. CBS plotted a $500,000 merchandising campaign during the sixties that exploited the characters in every type of toy, game, and salable item.

Merchandisers produced a miniature Clampett car, complete with character figurines that sat in the seat. This unique replica sold then for only a few dollars, while collectors now purchase the cars in good condition for several hundred dollars. Milburn Drysdale would have been ecstatic!

In addition, the Beverly Hillbillies were splashed all over bubblegum cards, comic books, a coloring book, jigsaw puzzles, a crayon-by-the-number portrait kit, T-shirts, pajamas, and board games. Moreover, the Elly May craze spawned a doll in her likeness,

OW, I HIT THE WRONG NAIL!!

GOT ANY SPARE PARTS FOR A 1921 TOURING CAR?

TODAY I BAGGED 2 SQUIRRELS AND A MINK COAT.

LET'S SHOOT SOMETHING FOR BREAKFAST

COURTESY OF STEPHEN COX

A series of Fleer Bubblegum cards was released with not-so-funny captions under the photos.

rope-tied jeans, and paper doll cutouts. If the public was a' buyin', CBS was a' sellin'!

Other items for sale included:

- The Hillbillies lunchbox and thermos (now averaging for nearly $20.00 to collectors.)
- Granny Halloween costume and mask.
- Whitman hardback storybook titled, *The Saga of Wildcat Creek*.
- View Master reels with a viewer and photo disk.
- A Beverly Hillbillies Bubble Pipe that kids could get from Kellogg's Cornflakes for twenty-five cents and one box top. The "corncob pipe" needed no soap—only water. "Shore is a heap o' fun!" the cereal box advertised.
- Model of the Hillbilly car, complete with character figurines.
- Rare collector postcards that the stars sent out to fans. These are being sought by aficionados.

Kids loved to bring the Hillbillies to school with them. Each colorful lunchbox also included a thermos. This item, in good shape, can fetch up to $50 today.

COURTESY OF STEPHEN COX

- Sheet music published for "The Ballad of Jed Clampett."
- A stereo album of songs by the cast with such "memorable" favorites as "A Long Talk with That Boy," sung by Jed and Jethro; "Jethro's a Powerful Man," and "Love of Money" warbled by Drysdale and Miss Jane.
- 8 × 10 glossy photos of the show's cast and scenes from the episodes. These generally run from $2.00 to $5.00 for black and white originals; color stills can cost up to $10.00 per photograph (1988 prices).

The harmony record album features songs by the cast. Note the misspelling of Kulp's name.

COURTESY OF STEPHEN COX

COURTESY OF STEPHEN COX

The Dell comic books were common items at one time but now run collectors from eight dollars to twenty dollars for a copy in mint condition.

Many of these items, sought by fans and couch-potatoes alike, pop up at flea markets, swap shops and TV/film conventions and are hidden in dusty attics across the country. Today, many of the items such as the 8 × 10 glossies and Hillbilly T-shirts are still being circulated, along with a few new items such as Hallmark's line of Hillbilly greeting cards. Each card is adorned with the faces of the stars and is appropriate for a variety of occasions. One card shows Granny holding her jug marked XXX. It reads: "It's Christmas, and as dear old Granny used to say when the family gathered around . . . 'Last one blitzed ain't tryin'!' " Another holiday greeting has Elly whistling to Jed, saying: "Wheeeoooooo! If you ain't the doggone-dapperest, hootie-owl-wisest, Sunday-best paw a gal ever had, I'll just spit! Happy Father's Day!"

COURTESY OF HALLMARK CARDS, INC.

Hallmark's line of Hillbilly greetings have proved successful in the card market.

Hillbilly Trivia

"Hillbilly trivia is some of the most frequently asked," says "Mr. Trivia" Dave Strauss, author, nationally recognized trivia master, and host of a popular call-in radio show on St. Louis's KMOX airwaves. "Did you know that Irene Ryan was one of Frank Capra's original choices for the role of the cook in *It's a Wonderful Life*?"

Here, for the simple fan and even the most ardent Granny buff, are some ticklers that will whet your Clampett appetite and possibly stump your scholarly memories. You can fetch the answers in the back of the book. Good Luck!

1. What was Granny's real name?
2. Dash Riprock dated who on the show . . . and what was his occupation and real name?
3. Who was the chairman of the board of The Commerce Bank of Beverly Hills? What actor, who also starred in Gilligan's Island, portrayed him?
4. Where was Granny born?
5. What was the name of the oil company that bought Jed's greasy swamp?
6. According to Granny, what kind of money was paid to Jed for the oil?
7. What was the Clampetts' address in Beverly Hills?
8. Who was the mayor of Bug Tussle?
9. Who was Granny's favorite movie star?
10. Jethro started his own restaurant called what?
11. What was the name of the biggest hotel in Bug Tussle?
12. What did cousin Roy (Roy Clark) try to peddle in Beverly Hills?
13. What was Granny's antidote to cousin Roy's merchandise?
14. What recovers Mr. Drysdale from a faint?
15. Name one of the favorite tunes of Bug Tussle.
16. Who did Granny beat to win the wrestling championship?
17. What was Sonny Drysdale's real name?
18. Who played cowboy hero Quirt Manley at Mammoth Studios?
19. How much allowance a week did Jethro receive?
20. Who was the series' announcer?
21. The Clampett mansion had how many rooms and baths?
22. Granny's daughter and Jed's deceased wife was named?
23. What was Jane Hathaway's middle name?
24. What was Elly May's full name?
25. In several episodes, Jed displayed a statue that he wittled. Who was the statue of?
26. What is Lootus Contractus?

27. Who sings the theme song, "The Ballad of Jed Clampett?"
28. What man directed the bulk of the Hillbilly episodes?
29. In the first few episodes, what was Jethro originally referred to as?
30. What cigarette brand was frequently advertised by the cast in specially tailored commercials in the early sixties?
31. The casts for what three shows got together for a Thanksgiving episode? (Hint: Hooterville.)
32. Who was Miss Jane always chasing after in the earlier episodes? Particular man, not just any man.
33. In *The Return of the Beverly Hillbillies*, what did Jed do to honor Granny, who had passed away?
34. What rendition does Jazzbo Depew sing to Jethrine?
35. What kind of hat did Jed wear for courting, and what was on the center of his good tie?
36. What is "Faversham!"?
37. Why did Mr. Drysdale grow a mustache?
38. What did Dr. Granny usually do for a head injury or sore?
39. Before going to England, Jed bought the deed to what country to present to the penniless Queen?
40. What did Cousin Pearl specialize in? (two answers—Hint: types of singing and playing.)

PHOTO BY GABI RONA

Television's Hillbilly family poses for a portrait that reflects their ratings. Weeelll, doggies, they're a hit!

7
EPISODE GUIDE

CAST

Buddy Ebsen..Jed Clampett
Irene Ryan..............................Granny (Daisy Moses)
Donna Douglas............................Elly May Clampett
Max Baer, Jr...............................Jethro Bodine
Raymond Bailey...........................Milburn Drysdale
Nancy Kulp........................Miss Jane Hathaway
Harriet MacGibbon.....................Margaret Drysdale
Bea Benaderet...............................Pearl Bodine
Larry Pennell................................Dash Riprock
Roger Torrey............................Mark Templeton
Elvia Allman............................Elverna Bradshaw
Sharon Tate....................................Janet Trego
Fred Clark................................Dr. Roy Clyburn
Milton Frome.............................Harry Chapman
Louis Nye.................................Sonny Drysdale
Max Baer, Jr..............................Jethrene Bodine
Linda Kaye Henning.....................Voice of Jethrene

First telecast: September 26, 1962
Last Telecast: September 7, 1971

The following is a complete list of every episode (168 color,
106 black and white). They are in order of their airing, by title.
A brief synopsis and a guest cast list have been included, along
with some additional sidelines and trivia regarding particular

episodes. For instance, you will notice Paul Henning frequently named his guest characters after real persons associated with the show, friends, and relatives. In one episode, Granny calls a pharmacy to order some backwoods ingredients for her remedies. She calls up Petey Childers back home. In reality, Pete Childers is Paul Henning's brother-in-law from Independence, Missouri, married to Paul's sister, Drusilla. Henning's relatives never knew what to expect when they tuned in.

PHOTO BY GABI RONA

Cruisin' the strip: Sunset strip, that is.
The Hillbillies arrive on the West Coast.

1. The Hillbillies of Beverly Hills (Pilot)
Jed Clampett sells his swamp full of oil to the O.K. Oil Company for $25 million and moves to Beverly Hills to live in a mansion.

Bea Benaderet.............................Cousin Pearl
Frank Wilcox...........Mr. Brewster, President, O.K. Oil.
Bob Osborne.................................Jeffrey Taylor
Ron Hagerthy....................................Geologist

2. Getting Settled
Wealthy Jed Clampett and his family are mistaken for a staff of backwoods servants when they arrive at their mansion.

3. Meanwhile, Back at the Cabin
The Clampetts find that the luxuries of their new mansion are a poor substitute for the comforts of their former mountain shack.

Bea Benaderet.............................Pearl Bodine
Frank Wilcox.................................Mr. Brewster
Max Baer, Jr...........................Jetherene Bodine
                    (Voice by Linda Kaye Henning)

4. The Clampetts Meet Mrs. Drysdale
When Mr. Drysdale describes his wife as a hypochondriac, the Clampetts assume she must be a tippler.

Harriet MacGibbon........................Mrs. Drysdale

5. Jed Buys Stock
When Drysdale advises the Clampetts to invest in stock, Jed rushes to buy some cows, pigs, goats, and chickens— livestock!

Arthur Gould Porter..............Ravenswood, the Butler
Sirry Steffen.............................Marie, the Maid

6. Trick or Treat
The homesick Clampetts, unaware that it's Halloween night, decide to go calling on their Beverly Hills neighbors.

Bea Benaderet..Pearl
Phil Gordon.......................Jasper "Jazzbo" Depew
Teddy Eccles......................................Little Boy
Frank Wilcox.................................Mr. Brewster
Max Baer, Jr.........................Jetherene Bodine
                    (Voice by Linda Kaye Henning)
Shirley Mitchell................................Governess

7. The Servants
Milburn Drysdale attempts another step in the social renovation of the Clampetts by lending them his servants.

Arthur Gould Porter........................Ravenswood
Sirry Steffen...Marie

8. Jethro Goes to School

Jed enrolls Jethro in the Millicent-Schuyler-Potts private school. Mrs. Potts, the private teacher, is surprised to find out her new student is Jethro.

Bea Benaderet.....................................Pearl
Eleanor Audley..............................Mrs. Potts
Phil Gordon....................Jasper "Jazzbo" Depew
Frank Wilcox.............................Mr. Brewster
Lisa Davis......................................Diana

COURTESY OF FILMWAYS

Elly May is not impressed by Sonny Drysdale (Louis Nye).

9. Elly's First Date

Elly May's first date with Mr. Drysdale's stepson, Sonny, ends in confusion before it even starts.

Harriet MacGibbon.........................Mrs. Drysdale
Louis Nye................................Sonny Drysdale

10. Pygmalion and Elly

Debonair Sonny Drysdale plays Pygmalion and Julius Caesar as he resumes his tempestuous courtship of the ingenuous Elly May.

Harriet MacGibbon.........................Mrs. Drysdale
Louis Nye................................Sonny Drysdale

11. Elly Races Jetherene

The Clampetts try to get Sonny to propose to Elly May before Cousin Pearl can get her hulky daughter, Jetherene, married to Jazzbo Depew.

Bea Benaderet.............................Cousin Pearl
Louis Nye................................Sonny Drysdale
Phil Gordon.................................Jasper Depew
Max Baer, Jr........................Jetherene Bodine
(Voice by Linda Kaye Henning)

12. The Great Feud

The Clampetts load up their shootin' irons for a march on the Drysdale estate after Sonny Drysdale jilts Elly May.

Sirry Steffen............................Marie, the Maid
Arthur Gould Porter.............Ravenswood, the Butler
Ken Drake....................................Psychiatrist
Lyle Talbot..............................2nd Psychiatrist

13. Home for Christmas

The Clampetts take their first airplane ride, returning to their mountain cabin for a surprise visit with Cousin Pearl.

Bea Benaderet......................................Pearl
Paul Winchell.............................Grandpa Winch
Frank Wilcox..............................Mr. Brewster
Jeanne Vaughn...................1st Airline Stewardess
Eilene Janssen...................2nd Airline Stewardess

14. No Place Like Home

The Clampetts, home for the holidays, help Cousin Pearl attract Mr. Brewster, the oil company executive.

Bea Benaderet......................................Pearl
Paul Winchell.............................Homer Winch
Frank Wilcox..............................Mr. Brewster

15. Jed Rescues Pearl

Pearl's efforts to snag the elusive Mr. Brewster seem doomed to failure, until he makes a ridiculous public marriage proposal.

Bea Benaderet......................................Pearl
Elvia Allman..........................Elverna Bradshaw
Frank Wilcox..............................Mr. Brewster

COURTESY OF PHIL GORDON

Character actor Phil Gordon with Bea Benaderet at the cabin set during one of the early episodes.

16. Back to Californy
Jed is confronted with too many cooks and not enough vittles when he invites Cousin Pearl and Jetherene to his Beverly Hills home.

Bea Benaderet.....................................Pearl
Phil Gordon...............................Jasper Depew
Frank Wilcox...............................Mr. Brewster
Gloria Marshall.......................Airline Stewardess
Max Baer, Jr...........................Jetherene Bodine
(Voice by Linda Kaye Henning)

17. Jed's Dilemma
Trying to cool a feud between Granny and Pearl, Jed takes his family on a sightseeing tour of Beverly Hills.
Bea Benaderet..Pearl

18. Jed Saves Drysdale's Marriage

Mr. Drysdale's marriage is threatened when he looks to the Clampetts for a housekeeper while his wife visits a health farm.

Bea Benaderet.....................................Pearl
Harriet MacGibbon.........................Mrs. Drysdale

19. Elly's Animals

Policemen and Elly May's animal friends converge on the Clampett estate when Cousin Pearl starts giving lessons in yodeling.

Bea Benaderet.....................................Pearl
Harriet MacGibbon.........................Mrs. Drysdale
Eddie Dean...............................1st Policeman
Peter Leeds..Joe
Brian Kelly.............................2nd Policeman
Karl Lukas..Frank

A police officer (Brian Kelly) dispatched to the Clampetts to investigate some smog (Granny's still) becomes infatuated with Elly May at first glance.

20. Jed Throws a Wingding

Two of Cousin Pearl's most ardent former suitors, Flatt and Scruggs, come to visit her in Beverly Hills.

Bea Benaderet....................................Pearl
Earl Scruggs....................................Himself
Lester Flatt....................................Himself
Midge Ware..................Louise Scruggs, Earl's wife
Joi Lansing..................Gladys Flatt, Lester's wife

21. Jed Plays Solomon

Granny's campaign to stop Pearl's yodeling backfires when Granny calls the law and the police find Granny's illegal still.

Bea Benaderet....................................Pearl
Eddie Dean....................................Sgt. Dean
Brian Kelly..................................Officer Kelly
Lucille Star.....................................Yodeler

22. Duke Steals a Wife

Duke, Jed's trusty bloodhound, becomes a matchmaker for his master and Mademoiselle Denise, a glamorous French woman.

Bea Benaderet....................................Pearl
Harriet MacGibbon........................Mrs. Drysdale
Narda Onyx..................................Mlle. Denise

23. Jed Buys the Freeway

A confidence man tries to sell Jed the Hollywood Bowl, Griffith Park, and the Hollywood Freeway.

Bea Benaderet....................................Pearl
Jesse White................................H. H. H. Jones
Dick O'Shea............................Auto Salesman

Jed, in his slickest outfit yet, gets a whistle outta Elly May.

COURTESY OF VIACOM

24. Jed Becomes a Banker

Jed Clampett is made a bank vice president so he can compete in an interbank skeet shoot for Mr. Drysdale, who lacks a partner.

Charles Lane.....................................Mr. Hacker
Lester Matthews...........................Mr. Pendleton
Jack Boyle...............................Photographer
Laura Shelton..............................Secretary

25. The Family Tree

An authority on early American history finds evidence that Jed Clampett's ancestors preceded the Mayflower to America.

Bea Benaderet......................................Pearl
Harriet MacGibbon.......................Mrs. Drysdale
Rosemary DeCamp.........................Mrs. Standish

26. Jed Cuts the Family Tree

Cousin Pearl gets a glamour treatment and tries to groom the Clampetts for their new status in high society.

Bea Benaderet......................................Pearl
Harriet MacGibbon.......................Mrs. Drysdale
Rosemary DeCamp.........................Mrs. Standish

27. Granny's Spring Tonic

Jed takes a double dose of Granny's spring tonic and winds up on Lovers Lane with a gold-digging bank secretary.

Bea Benaderet......................................Pearl
Lola Albright..............................Gloria Buckles
(Gloria Buckles was Paul Henning's secretary.)

28. Jed Pays His Income Tax

An IRS agent calls on the Clampetts and gets a roaring shotgun welcome from Granny.

Bea Benaderet......................................Pearl
Frank Wilcox..................................Mr. Brewster
John Stephenson...........................Mr. Landman
Ron Hagerthy....................................Geologist

29. The Clampetts and the Dodgers

Los Angeles Dodger coach Leo Durocher can't believe his eyes when he sees Jethro throw a baseball with such speed and accuracy.

Leo Durocher......................................Himself
Wally Cassell..............................Buzzie Bavasi
Skip Ward....................................Walsh Wesson
Norman Leavitt.................................Attendant

30. Duke Becomes a Father
Love looms again for Jed when the glamorous Mlle.
Denise returns from Paris to herald the arrival of a new
litter of puppies.
Harriet MacGibbon.........................Mrs. Drysdale
Narda Onyx..................................Mlle. Denise

31. The Clampetts Entertain
The board chairman of the Commerce Bank of Beverly
Hills is determined to meet the bank's "ace financial
wizard" and largest depositor, tycoon Jed Clampett.
Harriet MacGibbon.........................Mrs. Drysdale
Jim Backus.........................Marty Van Ransohoff
(Marty Ransohoff was the chairman of the board for
Filmways Television, owners of the show.)

Granny wonders whether
Mrs. Drysdale's stole would
be fittin' fer dinner.

COURTESY OF VIACOM

32. The Clampetts in Court

Jed acts as his own attorney when he's sued by an unscrupulous couple seeking $100,000 damages for a fictitious traffic accident.

Kathleen Freeman.........................Mabel Johnson
Murvyn Vye..............................James Johnson
Roy Roberts...................................Judge
Dean Harens................................Attorney
Jess Kirkpatrick...............................Bailiff

33. The Clampetts Get Psychoanalyzed

The Clampetts have a series of unusual encounters with a Beverly Hills psychiatrist.

Bea Benaderet....................................Pearl
Herbert Rudley...........................Dr. Twombly
Dick Wesson..................................Patient
Karen Norris....................................Nurse
(The real Gene Twombly was Bea Benarderet's husband)

34. The Psychiatrist Gets Clampetted

A Beverly Hills psychiatrist pursues Granny instead of Pearl when Granny's secret love charm misfires.

Bea Benaderet....................................Pearl
Herbert Rudley...........................Dr. Twombly

35. Elly Becomes a Secretary

Jed Clampett takes over Milburn Drysdale's job for one afternoon and wins for him the title of "Banker of the Year."

John Ashley............................Bob Billington
Willis Bouchey.............................Mr. Willis
Patty Jo Harmon................................Kitty
Bill Baldwin.....................Convention Speaker

36. Jethro's Friend

The Clampetts take a pampered eleven-year-old boy in to show him how to really enjoy himself.

Hayden Rorke..................................Wilkins
Michel Petit.............Armstrong Dueser McHugh III
(Armstrong, Dueser & McHugh was the name of the public relations firm that handled some of the cast.)

37. Jed Gets the Misery

To humor Granny, Jed fakes illness so that she can resume the doctoring practice that brought her fame in the hills.

Fred Clark..................................Dr. Clyburn

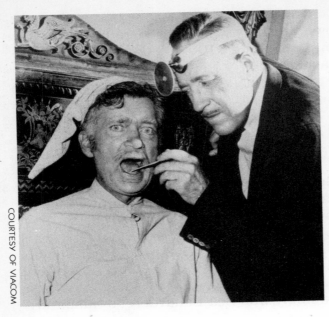

COURTESY OF VIACOM

Dr. Roy Clyburn, played by Fred Clark, was known as the "healer with a heart" with an office in the Crestview Medical Building. The Beverly Hills physician detested Granny's mountain medicine.

38. Hair-Raising Holiday

Granny defies medical opposition to her own brand of mountain medicine as she reveals an astonishing ability to grow hair.

Fred Clark..................................Dr. Clyburn

39. Granny's Garden

Her neighbors are aghast when Granny decides to start a vegetable garden on the grounds of the Clampett mansion.

40. Elly Starts to School

Elly May sparks a new trend in understated fashion when she enrolls at a finishing school for pampered rich girls.

Harriet MacGibbon........................Mrs. Drysdale
Doris Packer...............................Mrs. Fenwick
Sharon Tate......................................Sharon
Joanna Barnes........................Cynthia Fenwick
Tom Cound..Beasley

41. The Clampett Look

Dressed as backwoods hillbillies, Cynthia Fenwick and her mother call on the Clampetts, thinking they are the new avant garde social leaders.

Doris Packer...............................Mrs. Fenwick
Joanna Barnes........................Cynthia Fenwick

42. Jethro's First Love

Jethro, after a man-to-man talk with Jed, wastes no time in finding a girlfriend who is a brassy burlesque dancer.

Barbara Nichols.................................Chickadee
Sharon Tate..................................Janet Trego

43. Chickadee Returns

Love-struck Jethro decides he wants to marry Chickadee Laverne, a brassy burlesque dancer he has brought home.

Barbara Nichols.................................Chickadee
Sharon Tate..................................Janet Trego

44. The Clampetts Are Overdrawn

Jed Clampett receives the startling news that his multimillion dollar account is overdrawn in the amount of $34.70.

King Donovan.....................Jake "J.D." Clampett
Shirley Mitchell...........................Opal Clampett
Sharon Tate..................................Janet Trego
Gil Perkins....................................Pool Man
Robert Foulk..................................Policeman
Jack Boyle..................................Photographer
Dick Crockett..................................Paving Man

COURTESY OF FILMWAYS

Penniless actor Jake Clampett (King Donovan), posing as a famous movie star cousin of Jed's, makes an effort to bilk Jed out of his fortune—not an unusual problem for the naive millionaire.

45. The Clampetts Go Hollywood
The Clampetts, under the noxious influence of J. D.
Clampett—imposter and unemployed actor—go
Hollywood in a big way.

King Donovan............................Jake Clampett
Shirley Mitchell...........................Opal Clampett
Sharon Tate................................Janet Trego

46. Turkey Day
Plans for a holiday feast at the Clampett mansion go
awry when Elly May makes a pet of the dinner.

Harriet MacGibbon........................Mrs. Drysdale
Benny Rubin..................................1st Indian
George Sawaya................................2nd Indian

47. The Garden Party
Mrs. Drysdale, giving a lavish garden party, finds, to her
horror, that she is losing her guests to the lively,
moonshine-serving Clampetts next door.

COURTESY OF VIACOM

Unfortunately, Mrs. Drysdale's party has shifted locations as the guests drift over to
the Clampett's for possum sandwiches and spiked punch.

Harriet MacGibbon.........................Mrs. Drysdale
Arthur Gould Porter........................Ravenswood
Curt Massey................................Violinist
Murray Pollock............................Young Man
Sharon Tate................................Young Girl
(Curt Massey recorded all of the background music for
the show.)

48. Elly Needs a Maw
Jed decides that his tomboy daughter Elly, who has taken
up motorcycle riding, needs a mother to make her a lady.
Doris Packer..............................Mrs. Fenwick
Sharon Tate...............................Janet Trego
Tom Cound..................................Beasley

49. The Clampetts Get Culture
The Clampetts try unsuccessfully to participate in some
of the more civilized pleasures of Beverly Hills.
Harriet MacGibbon.........................Mrs. Drysdale
Eleanor Audley..............................Mrs. Potts
Sharon Tate...............................Janet Trego
Don Orlando...............................Italian Tailor

50. Christmas at the Clampetts
Christmas Day finds the Clampetts befuddled by their
expensive gifts, all from Mr. Drysdale.
Harriet MacGibbon.........................Mrs. Drysdale
Arthur Gould Porter........................Ravenswood

51. A Man for Elly
Quirt Manly, celebrated star of TV westerns, is invited to
the Clampett mansion to try to tame Elly May.
Henry Gibson...............................Quirt Manly
Amedee Chabot.................................Girl

52. The Giant Jackrabbit
An Australian banker sends Drysdale a kangaroo as a
joke and Granny thinks she has discovered a giant
jackrabbit.
Arthur Gould Porter........................Ravenswood
Sharon Tate...............................Janet Trego
Peter Bourne.............................Bill Tinsman
Kathy Kersh...........................Marian Billington
(This episode, airing January 8, 1964, received a 44.0
percent share and remains the highest rated half-hour
show since 1960, when Nielsen changed its rating
system. It altered television history.)

53. The Girl from Home
A young beauty contest winner from back home and her father come to visit Jethro with marriage on their minds.
Muriel Landers.....................................Essiebelle
Peter Whitney.......................................Lafe Crick
Chet Stratton..........................Jewelry Salesman
Kathy Kersh..........................Marian Billington

54. Lafe Lingers On
Backwoods freeloader Lafe Crick lingers at the Clampetts' mansion as an unwanted guest in search of easy fortune.
Peter Whitney.................................Lafe Crick

55. The Race for Queen
Elly May Clampett enters—and almost wins—the Miss Beverly Hills beauty contest.
Bob Cummings...............................Himself
Susan Hart.....................................Candy Davis
Harriet MacGibbon.........................Mrs. Drysdale
Kathy Kersh...........................Marian Billington

56. The Critter Doctor
Granny gets her dander up when she confuses an insecticide salesman with a "critter doctor" Elly May has called.
Mark Goddard...............................Jim Gardner
Russell Collins..............................Dr. Martin

57. Lafe Returns
Still trying to get his hands on the Clampett loot, Lafe Crick returns, ostensibly to give Granny a pawpaw tree.
Peter Whitney..............................Lafe Crick
Bobs Watson................................Fred Penrod

58. Son of Lafe Returns
Lafe Crick brings his hillbilly son, Dub, to Beverly Hills to court Elly May.
Peter Whitney..............................Lafe Crick
Conlan Carter...............................Dub Crick
Bobs Watson................................Fred Penrod

59. The Clampetts Go Fishing
The Clampetts embark on an unusual fishing trip at the famed Marineland of the Pacific.
Mark Tapscott..........................Marine Sergeant
Glen Stensel.......................Air Force Lieutenant

60. A Bride for Jed

Jane Hathaway comes up with a unique idea of how to find a wife for Jed Clampett, with disastrous results.

Earl Scruggs....................................Himself
Midge Ware...............................Mrs. Scruggs
Joi Lansing...................................Mrs. Flatt
Adele Clair...................................Contestant

61. Granny Versus the Weather Bureau

Granny's old-fashioned ways of predicting the weather are pitted against the Weather Bureau's advanced technology. She uses Cecil, her weather-beetle.

Quinn O'Hara...............................Weather Girl
Helen Kleeb.........................Addison's Secretary
John McGiver.........................Judson Addison

62. Another Neighbor

Several of Beverly Hills's more prominent citizens are more than a little affected when they sample Granny's spring tonic.

Harriet MacGibbon.....................Mrs. Drysdale
Jean Willes.........................Countess Maria
Susan Hart.............................Candy Davis
Burt Mustin...............................Chauffeur

63. The Bank Raising

Invited to the dignified ground-breaking for a new bank, the Clampetts confuse the event with an old-fashioned "barn raisin'."

Lester Matthews.......................Mr. Pendleton
Bill Baldwin..............................Bill Baldwin
Addison Richards...........................Mr. Lucas
Kathy Kersh.........................Marian Billington

64. The Great Crawdad Hunt

Two Beverly Hills tycoons continue to probe the mysterious doings of that inscrutable financial wizard, J. D. Clampett.

Peter Leeds...............................Harry Sledge
Addison Richards...........................Mr. Lucas
Lester Matthews.......................Mr. Pendleton

65. The Dress Shop

The Clampetts, on the advice of Mr. Drysdale, become the owners of the most exclusive dress shop in Beverly Hills.

Natalie Schafer.........................Madame Renee
Marjorie Bennett.......................Mrs. Langwell

66. The House of Granny

The Clampetts' new exclusive dress shop becomes "The House of Granny"—complete with cracker barrel and a potbellied stove.

Ray Kellogg...................................Policeman
Maurice Marsac................................Doorman
George Cisar............................Police Sergeant
Edna Skinner...............................Mrs. Wright

67. The Continental Touch

Snooty Mrs. Drysdale mistakes Elly May for a European princess and excitedly plans a lavish party in her honor.

Harriet MacGibbon.........................Mrs. Drysdale
Janine Grindel............................Madame Potvin
Maurice Marsac.................................Maurice

68. Jed, Incorporated

Jed does business in his own way when Drysdale forms Clampco, Inc. as a tax shelter and makes Jed president.

69. Granny Learns to Drive

Granny, after a taxi ride, thinks the driver is trying to get fresh with her and take advantage of her. She decides she wants to learn to drive.

Mel Blanc.........................Cabbie, Dick Burton
Harry Lauter.............................Motorcycle Cop
(This was a rare on-screen appearance by Mel Blanc, the voice of Bugs Bunny and Porky Pig, and many other cartoon characters.)

70. Cabin in Beverly Hills

Banker Drysdale's remedy for Granny's homesickness starts the first social revolution in the history of Beverly Hills.

Sheila James............................Ginny Jennings
John Stephenson.......................Professor Graham
Harriet MacGibbon.........................Mrs. Drysdale
Jack Bannon..Man
(Jack Bannon is the son of actress Bea Benaderet.)

71. Jed Foils a Home Wrecker

Jed and Drysdale foil Mrs. Drysdale's plan to tear down the cabin her husband built for Granny on the Clampett estate.

Sheila James............................Ginny Jennings
John Stephenson.......................Professor Graham
Mike Ross................................Al Ledbetter

72. Jethro's Graduation
When Jethro misses his graduation from sixth grade, Skipper the chimp pinch-hits for him.
Eleanor Audley.................................Mrs. Potts
Mike Barton......................................Boy
Happy Derman.....................................Boy
Lisa Davis......................................Diana
Donald Foster........................Theodore Switzer
(Ted Switzer was a publicity man for the show.)

73. Jed Becomes a Movie Mogul
Jed Clampett becomes a confused movie mogul after his banker purchases the control of Mammoth Pictures Corporation.

74. Clampett City
Overjoyed to discover a rustic village on the back lot of the Mammoth Pictures studio, the Clampetts decide to settle there.
Sallie Janes..............................Miss Swenson
Milton Frome............................Larry Chapman
Russ Conway..................................Director
John Abbott.................................Sir Trevor
Alvy Moore......................................Alvin
Ray Kellogg...................................Gateman
(Alvy Moore went on to star as Hank Kimball in "Green Acres.")

75. Clampett City General Store
The Clampetts take part in a movie epic film produced by their studio, Mammoth Pictures.
Sallie Janes..............................Miss Swenson
Milton Frome............................Larry Chapman
Theodore Marcuse...............................Nero
Nestor Paiva...............................Auctioneer

76. Hedda Hopper's Hollywood
Hedda Hopper joins the battle against Drysdale's plan to destroy Mammoth Studios.
Hedda Hopper..................................Herself
Don Haggerty............................1st Policeman
Bill Baldwin..............................Bill Baldwin
Ted Fish...............................2nd Policeman

77. Doctor Jed Clampett

Granny suffers pangs of professional jealousy after Jed receives an honorary "doctor's" degree from Greely College.

Cully Richards	Bus Driver
Richard St. John	Dean Cromwell
Virginia Sale	Chicken Woman
Fabian Dean	Knife Thrower
Hazel Shermet	Mother
Tina Marie Brockert	Child
Roy Rogers	Fire Eater

78. Jed the Heartbreaker

In another effort to drive the uncouth Clampetts from Beverly Hills, the snobbish Mrs. Drysdale attempts a new tactic.

Harriet MacGibbon	Mrs. Drysdale

79. Back to Marineland

Anxious to do his hitch, Jethro heads for Marineland—to join the U.S. Marines.

Sharon Tate	Secretary
Robert Carson	Marineland Manager

80. Teenage Idol

Johnny Poke, singing idol of millions, has a hectic reunion with his old friends, the Clampetts.

Jesse Pearson	Johnny Poke

Granny brings a tel-ee-phone from back home and demands that a party line be installed—not fer yappin', just fer listenin'.

COURTESY OF VIACOM

81. The Widow Poke Arrives

In one of her periodic campaigns to get Jed married, Granny secretly summons an old and marriageable acquaintance.

Jesse Pearson	Johnny Poke
Susan Walther	1st Teenager
Alan Reed	Eddie Colton
Marie Elena	2nd Teenager

82. The Ballet

Mrs. Drysdale tries to enlist Jed Clampett's financial support for the struggling Beverly Hills Ballet Company.

Harriet MacGibbon	Mrs. Drysdale
Barrie Duffus	Ballerina
Leon Belasco	Victor Gregory

Milburn and Margaret Drysdale with their pet pooch, "Prince Claude of Burgundy."

COURTESY OF VIACOM

83. The Boarder
The Clampetts decide to rent out rooms, and their first boarder turns out to be Mrs. Drysdale's militarily efficient English butler.
Arthur Treacher.....................................Pinckney

84. The Boarder Stays
Pinckney, the English butler engaged to impart culture to the Clampetts, finds his job an uphill struggle all the way.
Arthur Treacher.....................................Pinckney

85. Start the New Year Right
Learning that Mrs. Drysdale is in the hospital because of a nervous ailment, the sympathetic hillbillies pay her a visit.
Harriet MacGibbon........................Mrs. Drysdale
Sue England....................................1st Nurse
Les Tremayne............................Dr. Stuyvesant
Jill Jarmyn....................................2nd Nurse

86. Clampett General Hospital
Having "rescued" Mrs. Drysdale from the hospital, the Clampetts try their own brand of medicine on her ailing system.
Harriet MacGibbon........................Mrs. Drysdale
Jean Howell...Nurse
Willis Bouchey..............................Dr. Sanders

87. The Movie Starlet
Jethro falls desperately in love with a volatile young movie starlet and desperately wants to marry her. When she finds out his uncle owns the studio, Kitty Devine follows Jethro.
Sharon Farrell...............................Kitty Devine
William Newell.........................1st Gate Guard
Bernie Kopell..................Jerry Best, Kitty's Agent
Rodney Bell............................2nd Gate Guard

88. Elly in the Movies
Through a mix-up, Dash Riprock mistakes Jane Hathaway for his new leading lady, Elly May Clampett.
Bill Quinn...Tom Kelly
Sally Mills...1st Girl
Ann Henry..2nd Girl
Diane Bond.......................................3rd Girl
Marilee Summers.................................4th Girl

89. Dash Riprock, You Cad
Elly May loses her second movie star boyfriend to plain
Jane, whose mysterious power over men continues to
baffle the Clampetts.

Sharon Tate...................................Janet Trego
Jeff Davis.......................................Biff Steel
Dermot A. Cronin...............................Crunch
Kent Miller.....................................Tab Strong
Larry Pennell..............................Dash Riprock
Jack Bannon..............................Bolt Upright
Glenn Wilder...............................Race Burley
Murray Alper..............................Studio Driver

90. Clampett A-Go-Go
The Clampetts care for a madcap artist who wrecks his
car when he sees Elly May in a bathing suit.

Alan Reed, Jr.............................Sheldon Epps
Larry Pennell.............................Dash Riprock

91. Granny's Romance
Mr. Drysdale forces a playboy on his bank's board of
directors into courting Granny.

Sylvia Lewis......................................Phyllis
Kent Smith..........................Clifton Cavanaugh

92. Jed's Temptation
Granny practices what she intended to preach against
when she sets out to save Jed from the evils of gambling.

Sylvia Lewis......................................Phyllis
Iris Adrian..Wife
Don Rickles...Fred
Ralph Montgomery.................................Usher

93. Double Naught Jethro
Jethro gives up his ambition of becoming a brain
surgeon to take on the perils and pleasures of a spy.

Sharon Tate...................................Janet Trego
Joyce Nizzari.............................Mabel Slocum

94. Clampett's Millions
A rival banker spirits the Clampett millions from
Milburn Drysdale's loving care.

Roy Roberts...............................John Cushing
Joyce Nizzari.............................Mabel Slocum

Gun-totin' Granny makes
sure that Mr. Drysdale
doesn't cross her path.

COURTESY OF VIACOM

95. Drysdale's Dog Days
Banker Drysdale's ordeal with Granny continues, as she
insists on seeing the $11,000,000 that is her share of
Jed's fortune.
Harriet MacGibbon.........................Mrs. Drysdale
Grandon Rhodes....................................Judge
Steve Brodie.......................................Guard
John Day......................................Chauffeur

96. Brewster's Honeymoon
An oil company executive spends a strange honeymoon in
a mountain cabin in Beverly Hills, courtesy of the
Clampetts.
Frank Wilcox...............................Mr. Brewster
Lisa Seagram...........................Edythe Williams

97. Flatt, Clampett, and Scruggs
Granny suffers from homesickness—until two old
friends, Lester Flatt and Earl Scruggs, arrive in Beverly
Hills.
Earl Scruggs......................................Himself
Lester Flatt......................................Himself
Frank Scannell..........................Stage Manager

98. Jed and the Countess
Spring tonic time brings the Countess von Holstein back
for another visit with the Clampetts.
Jean Willes...............................Countess Maria
Burt Mustin...................................Humphrey

99. Big Daddy, Jed
Sheldon Epps, the extraordinary beatnik, pays a return
visit to the Clampetts to borrow "bread" from Jed.
Marianne Gaba................................Squirrel
Diki Lerner.....................................Wiggy
Paul De Rolf....................................Horace
Alan Reed, Jr............................Sheldon Epps
Keva Page.......................................Shaky

100. Cool School Is Out
Granny turns beatnik when she visits the Parthenon
West coffee house to rescue Elly May and Jethro from a
band of beatniks.
Marianne Gaba................................Squirrel
Diki Lerner.....................................Wiggy
Paul De Rolf....................................Horace
Alan Reed, Jr............................Sheldon Epps
Keva Page.......................................Shaky

101. The Big Bank Battle
Jed Clampett is offered a bank vice presidency—an
inducement to get him to move his millions to another
bank.
Roy Roberts..............................John Cushing
Sue Casey............................Roberta Grahman

102. The Clampetts Versus Automation
When a computer replaces one of Drysdale's bookkeepers,
the displaced worker finds real friends in the Clampetts.
Byron Foulge..............................Leroy Lester
Sharon Tate...............................Janet Trego

103. Luke's Boy
The arrival in Beverly Hills of a prize matrimonial
prospect for her granddaughter, Elly May, puts Granny in
a dither.
Pat Winters...............................Ann Gardner
Chanin Hale...............................Linda Curry
Robert Easton........................Beauregard Short
Edy Williams......................................Girl

104. The Brewsters Return

The Clampetts force their well-intentioned but crude hospitality upon oil man John Brewster and his cultured bride.

Frank Wilcox............................John Brewster
Hal Taggart............................Walter McKeegan
Lisa Seagram...........................Edythe Williams

105. Jed, the Bachelor

Granny, finally making good her threat to go home to the hills, takes to the road.

Peter Leeds...................................Truck Driver

Granny, dissatisfied with the swanky rich folk, packs her bags and heads for home. She makes it as far as Las Vegas.

Julie Van Zandt.............................Policewoman
Ray Kellogg...................................Policeman
La Rue Farlow.......................Woman with Purse

106. The Art Center
Painting and sculpturing, the Hillbillies produce a
ghastly collection of "art" works for a new Beverly Hills
art gallery.
Harriet MacGibbon.......................Mrs. Drysdale
Walter Woolf King..........................George Engle
Chet Stratten.................................Fredericks
Gay Gordon.......................................Model

107. Admiral Jed Clampett
Jed Clampett, wearing a vice admiral's uniform,
mistakes a U.S. Navy destroyer for a yacht his banker
wants him to buy.
Rick Cooper.....................................Ensign
Mark Evans.......................................Seaman
Frank Coghlin..................................Helmsman
Garrison True..................................Radarman
Ray Kellogg.....................Speedboat Operator
(This is the first episode of the fourth season and the
first episode shot in color.)

108. That Old Black Magic
Granny becomes convinced that Mrs. Drysdale has used
"black magic" to turn herself into a crow.
Harriet MacGibbon.......................Mrs. Drysdale
Dave Willock........................Elevator Starter
Tris Coffin...................................Psychiatrist
Allison McKay................................Receptionist
John Gallaudet.............................Veterinarian

109. The Sheik
A sheik from the Middle East gives Jed Clampett a
present of four dancing girls and then falls for Elly May.
Dan Seymour.......................................Sheik
Naji Gabbay...Aide
Charlotte Knight...............................Newshen
Frank Wilcox.....................................Brewster
Bill Baldwin.......................................Himself
Phil Gordon.......................................Reporter
Nai Bonet.................................Dancing Girls
Diane Bond
Marianne Case
Lisa Britton

COURTESY OF VIACOM

Dan Seymour, as a shiek, talks to Granny
about a possible induction into his harem.

110. The Private Eye
Jethro, whose ambition is to be a secret agent, winds up
an unwitting accomplice in a plot to burglarize
Drysdale's bank.
Donald Curtis....................................Banker
James Seay....................................Detective
Eileen O'Neill..Kay

111. Possum Day
Drysdale tries to arrange a Possum Day festival to keep
the Clampetts from going back home.
Harriet MacGibbon........................Mrs. Drysdale
Sharon Tate..................................Janet Trego

112. The Possum Day Parade
Banker Drysdale continues his frantic efforts to promote
a Possum Day Parade for the Clampetts.
Harriet MacGibbon........................Mrs. Drysdale
Barney Elmore.................................Chauffeur
Maurice Kelly..Man
Sharon Tate..................................Janet Trego
Bill Baldwin......................................Himself
Francisco Ortega.....................................Man

113. The Clampetts Play the Rams
Jethro discovers that it is his color television set and not him that has won the heart of the pretty next-door maid.
Nina Shipman.....................................Linda
Beecey Carlson....................................Cook

114. The Courtship of Elly
Granny distills a love potion intended to land a husband for her "decrepit" granddaughter, Elly May (she's past fourteen).
Van Williams...............................Dean Peters

115. A Real Nice Neighbor
Drysdale and Granny try to marry off Jed Clampett to a frumpy housemaid they have mistaken for a millionaire.
Kathleen Freeman.................................Agnes
William Bakewell.............................Chauffeur

116. The Poor Farmer
The Clampetts think a dieting billionaire is a starving farmer, and they try to fatten him up.
Sebastian Cabot......................Lucas Sebastian
Lester Matthews.............................Pendleton
Hal Baylor...Joe
William Forrest.................................Canady

117. Hoe Down A-Go-Go
The senior Clampetts plan an old-fashioned barn dance, but Elly May and Jethro turn it into a rock 'n' roll blast.
Paul De Rolf.........................Specialty Dancer
The Enemies................................Themselves

118. Mrs. Drysdale's Father
Mrs. Drysdale's father, a wily Bostonian short of cash, finds it is no easy matter to part the Clampetts from their loot.
Harriet MacGibbon.....................Mrs. Drysdale
Charlie Ruggles..............Lowell Reddings Farquhar
Arthur Gould Porter.........................Ravenswood

119. Mr. Farquhar Stays On
When Mr. Farquhar asks Granny to go to Las Vegas, she thinks he is proposing an elopement rather than a gambling spree.
Harriet MacGibbon.....................Mrs. Drysdale
Charlie Ruggles..............Lowell Reddings Farquhar

120. Military School
The Clampett estate becomes a battlefield when Jethro enrolls in an exclusive Beverly Hills military academy.

John Hoyt......................................Col. Hollis
Craig Hundley.......................................Cadet
John Reilly...................................Capt. Hogan

121. The Common Cold
Granny opens her own doctor's office when a doctor refuses to believe she has a cure for the common cold.

Lowell Reddlings Farquhar (Charlie Ruggles) doesn't seem at all disturbed by Jed's poker hand—four aces—because he's holding a straight flush in this scene from "Mrs. Drysdale's Father."

COURTESY OF FILMWAYS

Fred Clark.....................................Dr. Clyburn
Olan Soule.......................................Salesman
Tom Browne Henry.............................Parker
Lenore Kingston.............................Receptionist

122. The Richest Woman
The richest woman in the world meets some stiff opposition from Jed when she insists on buying the Clampett mansion.
Martha Hyer.............................Tracy Richards
Douglas Dumbrille.................................Doug

123. The Trotting Horse
The Hillbillies are unimpressed with the costly, champion harness-racing horse banker Drysdale buys for them as an investment.
Harriet MacGibbon.........................Mrs. Drysdale
Norman Leavitt....................................Driver
Herb Vigran.....................................Handler

124. The Buggy
Banker Milburn Drysdale persuades his wife to accept Granny's challenge to a horse-and-buggy race.
Harriet MacGibbon.........................Mrs. Drysdale

125. The Cat Burglar
A burglar on the loose in Beverly Hills tries to deceive the Clampetts before robbing their mansion.
John Ashley..................................Mike Wilcox
Norman Grabowski..................................Bernie

126. The Big Chicken
Granny discovers an ostrich gulping tomatoes in her backyard and thinks it's a giant chicken.
Harriet MacGibbon.........................Mrs. Drysdale
John Baer...Nelson
Arthur Gould Porter.........................Ravenswood

127. Sonny Drysdale Returns
Sonny Drysdale pays a return visit to Beverly Hills, rekindling the Clampetts' hopes of a marriage to Elly May.
Harriet MacGibbon.........................Mrs. Drysdale
Louis Nye..Sonny

COURTESY OF FILMWAYS

Sonny Drysdale flips head-over-heels for Elly May.

128. Brewster's Baby

Granny announces she is going back home on doctor business to "fetch" a baby into the world.

Lisa Seagram....................................Mrs. Brewster
Joyce Nizzari.......................................Kitty Kat
Christine Williams.......................................Girl
Frank Wilcox.......................................Brewster

129. The Great Jethro

A starving but flamboyant vaudeville magician sees in the gullibility of Jethro and his uncle Jed a chance to get rich quick.

Lennie Bremen..................................Truck Driver
Britt Nilsson...Girl
Carolyn Williams.......................................Girl
Al Eben.......................................Truck Driver

130. The Old Folks Home
Granny fears that her kin plan to send her to an old folks home when they suggest she'd be happier in a country cottage.
Edith Leslie...................................Mrs. Mack
Barney Elmore...................................Perkins

131. Flatt and Scruggs Return
Country music stars Lester Flatt and Earl Scruggs return for a song-filled visit to the Clampetts.
Lester Flatt....................................Himself
Joi Lansing................................Gladys Flatt
Earl Scruggs...................................Himself
Barney Elmore.................................Chauffeur

132. The Folk Singers
Jethro abandons his dangerous career as an "Astronaut" for the even more precarious one of the folksinger.
Tom D'Andrea.................................Kingsley
Venita Wolf................................Miss Murray

133. The Beautiful Maid
A glamorous Swedish actress who yearns to play a hillbilly moves in with the Clampetts to study backwoods dialect.
Julie Newmar.............................Ulla Bergstrom
Milton Frome..................................Chapman

134. Jethro's Pad
Girl-crazy Jethro concludes that he must have a cool bachelor "pad" in order to make a hit with the fair sex.
Bettina Brenna....................................Edy
Christine Williams.........................1st Kitty Kat
Phyllis Davis.............................2nd Kitty Kat

135. The Bird Watchers
A bird-watching professor jeopardizes Elly May's romance with film star Dash Riprock.
Wally Cox..............................Professor Biddle
Venita Wolf................................Miss Murray
Larry Pennell.............................Dash Riprock

COURTESY OF HOWARD ARCHIVES/FILMWAYS

Wally Cox is P. Caspar Bittle, the gentle leader of the Bittle Birdwatchers Society of Beverly Hills. Jane Hathaway is the Flockmaster in search of the condor.

136. Jethro Gets Engaged
Jethro is elated, sure he's going to be twice as big a movie star as Dash Riprock, when he lands a job as Dash's double.

Joan Huntington...........................Debbie Haber
Phil Gordon...........................Pat Harrington
Dick Winslow...Man
Larry Pennell...............................Dash Riprock
Ray Kellogg...Guard

137. Granny Tonics a Birdwatcher
Professor P. Caspar Biddle, the meek little leader of Biddle's Bird Watchers, guzzles Granny's annual spring tonic and turns into a tiger.

Wally Cox...............................Professor Biddle
Venita Wolf...............................Miss Murray

138. Jethro Goes to College
Jethro decides he's ready for college and enrolls in the only one that will accept him—a run-down secretarial school.

Louise Lorimer.................................Dean Frisby
Gloria Neil..................................Miss Plumpett
Hope Summers.............................Miss Pringle
Shuji J. Nozawa.........................Hoshu Fujiyama

139. The Party Line
Granny, who used to spend ten hours a day on her party line back home, demands a party-line phone in Beverly Hills, too.
Vinton Hayworth...................................Cramer

140. The Soup Contest
Granny hopes to win Elly May a husband by entering an old hillbilly dish in a recipe contest and signing Elly May's name to it.
Gavin Gordon............................Stafford Clark
Steve Dunne.........................Roger Dickerback
Steve Pendleton.............................Director

141. Jethro Takes Love Lessons
Jethro falls for a waitress, who gives him the brush-off until she learns he's a friend of handsome movie idol Dash Riprock.
Larry Pennell.........................Dash Riprock
Carol Booth....................................Susie

142. The Badger Game
Blackmailers use hidden photographic and recording devices to trap unsuspecting Jed Clampett.
Leon Ames............................Colonel Foxhall
Gayle Hunnicutt................................Emaline

143. The Badgers Return
Having failed in their attempt to fleece Jed Clampett, a pair of blackmailers turn their attention to banker Drysdale.
Leon Ames............................Colonel Foxhall
David Frankham.........................Lt. Richards
Gayle Hunnicutt................................Emaline

144. The Gorilla
Jethro shops around for a gorilla when Elly May's pet chimpanzee proves too small to relieve him of his household chores.
George Barrows...................................Gorilla

145. Come Back, Little Herby
The Clampetts beg banker Drysdale to arrange the
return of their gorilla chore-boy, Herby.
George Barrows............................Gorilla Kelly

146. Jed in Politics
Jed runs for Smog Commissioner when the incumbent
stops Granny from cooking up her smog-producing
homemade lye soap.
Paul Reed.......................................Tinsley

147. Clampett Cha Cha Cha
Marvin and Marita, impoverished exponents of the
dance, introduce the Clampetts to the art of terpsichore.
Frank Faylen...................................Marvin
Iris Adrian.....................................Marita

148. Jed Joins the Board
Millionaire Jed Clampett finds a job as a garbage
collector because he's weary of loafing.
Frank Wilcox..................................Brewster
Owen Cunningham.............................Director
Jack Grinnage................................Co-Pilot
Jan Arvan......................................Forbes
Barry Kelly...................................Brachner
Tommy Farrell...................................Pilot
Lindsay Workman.............................Peterson

149. Granny Lives It Up
Granny is pursued simultaneously by two elderly swains,
each of whom is after her money.
Harriet MacGibbon......................Mrs. Drysdale
Charlie Ruggles.............................Farquhar
Diane Farrell................................Page Girl
Jo Ann Pflug.................................Showgirl
Anne Newman.............................Showgirl #2
Roy Roberts..................................Cushing

150. The Gloria Swanson Story
The Clampetts arrange a career comeback for an idol of
the silent screen.
Gloria Swanson..............................Herself
George Neise...............................Auctioneer
Lennie Bremen..............................Mover #1
Frank Sully................................Mover #2
Milton Frome...............................Chapman
Ray Kellogg....................................Guard

151. The Woodchucks

Girl-crazy Jethro tries to join Biddle's Bird Watchers after he spots a beauty in the ranks of the for-women-only club.

Nancy Dow....................................Athena
Sandy Berke....................................Lolita
Jerry Rannow....................................Stanley

152. Foggy Mountain Soap

Recognizing the homespun sincerity of Jed and Granny, an advertising man persuades them to appear in a television soap commercial.

Flatt & Scruggs..............................Themselves
Bobs Watson..............................Henry Hogan
Tom Curtis..............................Makeup Man
Edward Andrews..............................Ratterman
Terry Phillips..............................Sound Man

153. The Christmas Present

The Clampetts broaden their Beverly Hills experience by working as temporary Christmas help in a department store.

Harriet MacGibbon..............................Mrs. Drysdale
James Millhollin..............................Manager
Bruce Hyde..............................Floorwalker
Dee Carroll..............................Woman

154. The Flying Saucer

Banker Drysdale hires three midgets the Montenaro brothers, to pose as men from outer space in a scheme to garner publicity for his bank.

Frank Delfino..............................1st Montenaro
Jerry Maren..............................2nd Montenaro
Billy Curtis..............................3rd Montenaro
John Alvin..............................Photographer

(The Montenaro characters were named after the show's property man, Joe Montenaro.)

155. The Mayor of Bug Tussle

The Clampetts are honored by a distinguished visitor from home—the mayor of Bug Tussle.

James Westerfield..............................Mayor Amos Hogg

156. Granny Retires
Banker Drysdale panics when Granny says that she's going to withdraw her fifteen million dollars from his bank and go back to the hills.
Fred Clark.....................................Dr. Clyburn

157. The Clampett Curse
Jed gives away the entire Clampett fortune to three struggling college girls, to Drysdale's horror.
Sheila James.............................Ginny Jennings
Toby Kaye.....................................Fran
Bernadette Withers...........................Lucy
Russ Grieve...........................Ranger Warkle

158. The Indians Are Coming
When some Indians claim part of the Clampett oil land, Granny prepares for an all-out war.
John Wayne..Himself
Vince St. Cyr.....................................Indian
Milton Frome...................................Chapman
John Considine.............................Little Fox
Stanley Waxman...................Chief Running Wolf

159. The Marriage Machine
The Hillbillies go a-courtin' by computer but only manage to misunderstand the choices of the electronic matchmaker.
Warrene King..............................Linda Oliver
Richard Collier................................Filbert
Larry Christman.................................Hugh
Lurene Tuttle.........................Gladys Peabody
John Ayres.......................................Bert

160. Elly Comes Out
Jed and Granny throw a "comin' out" party for Elly May, and Mrs. Drysdale plots to make the affair a fiasco.
Harriet MacGibbon........................Mrs. Drysdale
Jenifer Lea...............................Secretary
Robert Strauss...........................Society Sandy

161. The Matador
After watching lovely admirers engulf El Magnifico, the world's greatest matador, jealous Jethro takes up bullfighting.
Milton Frome...................................Chapman
Kay St. Germain................................Secretary
Miguel Landa..............................El Magnifico

162. The Gypsy's Warning
Mrs. Drysdale hires a pair of fortune tellers to frighten
the Clampetts out of Beverly Hills with dire prophecies.
Harriet MacGibbon.........................Mrs. Drysdale
Leon Belasco..Yerko
Bella Bruck...Narda

163. His Royal Highness
Ex-King Alexander of Sabalia tries to marry wealthy Elly
May Clampett because he really hasn't a nickel to his
name.
Jacques Bergerac.........................King Alexander
Edward Ashley..............................Man on Yacht
Victoria Carroll..................................Doreen

164. Super Hawg
The Clampetts acquire a hippopotamus when an advertising scheme originated by banker Drysdale backfires.

165. The Doctors
It's spring again and Granny tries to dispense her free
tonic at the bank—resulting in another run-in with Dr.
Clyburn.
Barbara Morrison.....................Mrs. De Longpre
Fred Clark......................................Dr. Clyburn
Lorraine Bendix..............................Miss Lovely

166. Delovely and Scruggs
Lester Flatt and Earl Scruggs revisit the Clampetts, and
Mrs. Flatt takes a screen test with Jethro acting as her
director.
Lester Flatt...Flatt
Earl Scruggs.....................................Scruggs
Joi Lansing.................................Gladys Flatt
Bobs Watson..............................Harry Hogan

167. The Little Monster
Banker Milburn Drysdale's precocious eleven-year-old
nephew swindles the Hillbillies out of all the valuable art
objects in their mansion.
Ted Ecoles...Milby

168. The Dahlia Feud
Mrs. Drysdale's attempt to grow prize-winning dahlias
renews her feud with Granny.
Harriet MacGibbon.........................Mrs. Drysdale
Ted Cassidy..Ted

169. Jed Inherits a Castle
The Clampetts learn that they have inherited a castle
and prepare for a journey to merry ole England.
Paul Lynde...................................Passport Clerk

170. The Clampetts in London
The Clampetts arrive in London where Granny
encounters difficulty with both the customs inspector
and an English "druggist."
Shary Marshall...........................Airline Hostess
Ernest Clarke..............................Giles Evans
John Orchard........................Customs Inspector
Alan Napier.....................................Chemist
Larry Blake...............................Cab Driver
Hugh Dempster.......................Cholmondeley
John Baron.....................................Chauffeur

171. Clampett Castle
The Clampetts arrive at their inherited English castle,
confusion reigns, and Jethro insists on acting like a
medieval knight.
John Baron....................................Chauffeur
Norman Claridge..............................Jenkins
Elaine Stevens...................................Maid
Alan Napier.....................................Chemist
Richard Caldicot..........................Faversham
Ernest Clarke.............................Giles-Evans
Sheila Fearn................................Young Lady

172. Robin Hood of Griffith Park
The Clampetts pay a $10 million tax on their castle in
England, turn the place over to the staff, and leave for
home.
Laurel Goodwin...................................Stella
Richard Caldicot..........................Faversham
John Baron....................................Chauffeur
Alan Reed, Jr....................................Buddy
Norman Claridge..............................Jenkins

173. Robin Hood and the Sheriff
Jethro continues to masquerade as the Robin Hood of
Griffith Park and draws the admiring allegiance of a
band of hippies.
Laurel Goodwin...................................Stella
Christian Anderson...............................Harold
Paul De Rolf......................................Paul

Pat McCaffrie...Fred
Alan Reed, Jr...Buddy
Carolyn Williamson...................................Ruthie
Victor French..Tony

174. Greetings from the President
When Jethro gets his draft notice, he buys himself a
surplus army tank and a general's uniform and begins
his own training.
Bea Benaderet..............................Cousin Pearl
Pat McCaffrie...Fred
Henry Corden...Charley

175. The Army Game.
Draftee Jethro's military career comes to a screeching
halt when Army psychiatrists refuse to believe his family
is for real.
Paul Reed...Col. Stark
Joe Conley...Sergeant
King Donovan...............................Psychiatrist

176. Mr. Universe Muscles In
A rival banker arranges a date for Elly May with a
handsome model, so Drysdale counters by furnishing
"Mr. Universe" as an escort.
Dave Draper...............................Mr. Universe
Roy Roberts.............................John Cushing
John Ashley..............................Troy Apollo

177. A Plot for Granny
Two confused salesmen attempt to sell Jed a cemetery
plot for a very much alive Granny.
Richard Deacon.............................Brubaker
Jesse White.......................................Mortimer

178. The Social Climbers
The Clampetts entertain a lady blacksmith, the social
leader of hillbilly society.
Harriet MacGibbon......................Mrs. Drysdale
Mary Wickes..........................Adeline Ashley
Gail Bonney.............................Mrs. Robinson

179. Jethro's Military Career
Bent on a military career, Jethro experiments with
underwater demolition while practicing to be a Navy
frogman in the swimming pool.

180. The Reserve Program

When Granny spies a group of movie actors dressed as Union soldiers, she prepares to go to war.

Lyle Talbot	Col. Blake
Bob Pickett	Lieutenant
Harry Fleer	Colonel
Ron Stokes	Sgt. O'Hara
William Mims	General Grant
Steve Thomas	Major

181. The South Rises Again

Granny recruits her own commandos against the Union when she thinks battle scenes for a Civil War movie are the real thing.

Lyle Talbot	Col. Blake
Harry Fleer	Colonel
Richard O'Shea	Sergeant
Harry Lauter	Captain
William Mims	Gen. Grant
Terry Phillips	Foster Phinney

(The real Foster Phinney was the show's assistant director.)

Granny dons Civil War garb for an espionage campaign against General Grant and his staff.

COURTESY OF VIACOM

182. Jethro in the Reserve

Granny thinks she has captured Gen. Ulysses S. Grant and sets out to woo him by donning a bathing suit.

Lyle Talbot...Col. Blake
William Mims.......................................Gen. Grant

183. Cimarron Drip

Jethro can't get himself a part in a television series, but Elly May's pet ape wins the starring role.

Larry Pennell......................................Dash Riprock
Theodore Marcuse...................................Von Schlepper
Milton Frome.......................................Larry Chapman
Jim Hayward..Maintenance Man

184. Corn Pone Picassos

Granny paints a picture to help Mrs. Drysdale win the Beverly Hills Culture Committee Award.

Harriet MacGibbon..................................Mrs. Drysdale
David Bond...Judge Curtis
Chet Stratton......................................A. Allen Allen
Frank Richards.....................................Truck Driver

185. The Clampetts Play Cupid

Granny quits trying to persuade Elly May to marry movie star Dash Riprock and decides to help plain Jane Hathaway hook him.

Larry Pennell......................................Dash
Valerie Hawkins....................................Camille Zoftick

186. The Housekeeper

Despite Granny's protests, Jed and banker Drysdale hire a housekeeper who quickly gets on Granny's nerves.

Fran Ryan..Miss Meek

187. The Diner

Jethro becomes the operator of a dilapidated diner when Jed Clampett decides to set his nephew up in the restaurant business.

Joan Huntington....................................Lois

188. Topless Anyone?

Jethro adopts a "topless" policy at his diner—by removing the caps from himself and his waitress, Elly May.

Ysable MacCloskey..................................Mrs. Vanderpont
James F. Stone.....................................Mr. Vanderpont
Robert Foulk.......................................Truck Driver
Venita Wolf..Secretary Suzy

189. The Great Snow
Granny gets homesick for the sight of snow, and Mr. Drysdale arranges for a blizzard to hit Beverly Hills.
Harriet MacGibbon..........................Mrs. Drysdale

190. The Rass'lin Clampetts
Granny's fighting mood is inflamed by a woman's wrestling match on television, and she joins the fray.
Harriet MacGibbon..........................Mrs. Drysdale
Jerry Randall (in drag)............Boston Strong Girl
Gene Lebell...Referee
Bill Baldwin.......................................Announcer
Gayle Caldwell...................................Rebecca

The Clampetts in a tag-team wrestling match:
Grapplin' Granny and her family vs. The Boston Strong Girl and her family. As expected, Elly and Granny whomp 'em.

COURTESY OF VIACOM

Granny has a stronghold on her opponent (Mike Mazurki) and does her share as part of a tag-team match.

191. The Great Tag-Team Match

The Hillbillies grid for a tag-team wrestling match after Granny defeats the Boston Strong Girl.

Alan Reed.....................................Gene Booth
Jerry Randall (in drag)................Boston Strong Girl
Kay St. Germain..................................Secretary
Mike Mazurki......................................Wrestler
Gayle Caldwell......................................Rebecca
Bill Baldwin.......................................Announcer

192. Jethro Proposes

Because she feels sorry about the lack of romance in Jane Hathaway's life, Granny forces Jethro to propose, expecting Jane to refuse.

Lisa Todd..Ilse
Friz Feld...Walter

193. The Clampetts Fiddle Around
Banker Drysdale hires the world's greatest violin
virtuoso to teach Jethro to play the fiddle.
Hans Conreid....................................Stromboli
Foster Brooks.............................."Fiddlin" Sam

194. The Soap Opera
Granny thinks a soap opera program is real and sets out
to rescue an actor patient who is about to undergo a
serious operation.
Grandon Rhodes..................................Doctor
Beecey Carlson....................................Maggie

195. Dog Days
Granny becomes enraged when Elly May's herd of canine
friends trample her every time she announces a meal is
ready.
Harriet MacGibbon.........................Mrs. Drysdale
Lisa Todd...Ilse

COURTESY OF VIACOM

Nearly five hundred animals were used on the series. Here, Elly has her hands full.

196. The Crystal Gazers
Granny convinces herself that she has the gift of prophecy and starts making doubtful predictions for her family and friends.
Connie Sawyer....................................Elverna

197. From Rags to Riches
Granny plans the first head transplant in history when banker Drysdale is hurt in a fracas with his wife.
Harriet MacGibbon........................Mrs. Drysdale
Carolyn Nelson...................................Secretary

198. Cousin Roy
Cousin Roy Halsey arrives from the hills as advance man for Granny's hated rival, Myrtle Halsey, noted distiller of "medicine."
Roy Clark............................Roy/Mother Myrtle
Phil Arnold..........................Maintenance Man
Peter Leeds...................................Policeman
(Jim Halsey is Roy Clark's manager.)

Mother Myrtle (Roy Clark) makes maniacal music while Jed cringes at the sound.

COURTESY OF FILMWAYS

199. A Bundle for Britain
Jed decides to withdraw his $80 million from Drysdale's bank and give it to "poverty stricken" England.
Richard Caldicott.............................Faversham
Ben Wrigley..................................Footman
Alan Mowbray................................Montrose

200. Something for the Queen
The Clampetts invade England again to visit their castle and to give Canada (which they have purchased) to the Queen.
Richard Caldicott.............................Faversham
Warrene Ott.................................Stewardess
Dick Wesson.............................Man on Plane
Mark Harris.......................Customs Inspector
Jack Bannon......................Customs Assistant
Brian Peck...................................Chauffeur

201. War of the Roses
Drysdale orders his secretary, Jane, to pose as Queen Elizabeth I, who the Hillbillies think is still England's ruler.
Richard Caldicott.............................Faversham
Sydney Arnold.................................Retainer
Rosalind Kight.................................Vanessa
William Kendall..........................Col. Dumbarton
Donald Bisset....................................Tetley
Peter Myers......................................Osgood

202. Coming Through the Rye
Jethro falls for a beautiful Scot, but his hillbilly kin confuse her with her hulking brother in a kilt and think Jethro is crazy.
Richard Caldicott.............................Faversham
Ilona Rodgers.....................................Sandy
William Kendall..........................Col. Dumbarton
Dave Prowse......................................Emlyn

203. Ghost of Clampett Castle
Banker Drysdale arranges for the "ghost" to scare the Clampetts out of their English castle and home to Beverly Hills.
Richard Caldicott.............................Faversham

204. Granny Goes to Hooterville
Granny plans a trip to Hooterville but gets sidetracked when she thinks that Jed is planning to marry Jane Hathaway.

Edgar Buchanan............................Joe Carson
Aron Kincaid.....................................Cliff
Frank Cady............................Sam Drucker

205. The Italian Cook
Jethro hires a cook, a gorgeous Italian girl who cooks
masterfully but doesn't know a word of English.
Maria Natonini...................................Maria
Mike Minor......................................Steve Elliot
Linda Kaye Henning...........................Betty Jo
Frank Cady............................Sam Drucker

206. The Great Cook-Off
Jethro begins dressing and acting like the noblest
Roman of them all to win the hand of Maria, the
beautiful Italian cook.
Maria Mirka.......................................Maria

207. Bonnie, Flatt, and Scruggs
The Hillbillies get to play the part of gangsters when Mr.
Drysdale makes a commercial film for his bank.
Lester Flatt....................................Himself
Joi Lansing...................................Gladys Flatt
Earl Scruggs..................................Himself
Percy Helton..............................Homer Cratchit

208. The Thanksgiving Spirit
The Hillbillies travel to Hooterville to spend
Thanksgiving with their friends from "Petticoat
Junction" and "Green Acres."
Lori Saunders..................................Bobbie Jo
Linda Kaye Henning...........................Betty Jo
Frank Cady............................Sam Drucker
Eddie Albert............................Oliver Douglas
Eva Gabor..................................Lisa Douglas
Tom Lester...Eb
Edgar Buchanan............................Uncle Joe
Meredith MacRae..............................Billie Jo
Mike Minor.......................................Steve
June Lockhart.........................Dr. Janet Craig

209. The Courtship of Homer Noodleman
Banker Drysdale has Dash Riprock pose as farm-boy
Homer Noodleman and try to win Elly May.
Frank Cady............................Sam Drucker
Larry Pennell...........................Dash Riprock
Tom Lester...Eb

210. The Hot-Rod Truck
Jethro tells Jed and Granny they're no longer "with it" and trades the old family jalopy for a new and powerful hot rod.
Georgene Barnes...................................Jeanie
Lonnie Burr................................Medicine Man

211. The Week Before Christmas
The Hillbillies head for a Christmas in Hooterville—and a possible wedding for Granny and Sam Drucker.
Lori Saunders...................................Bobbie Jo
Frank Cady................................Sam Drucker
Meredith MacRae...............................Billie Jo

212. Christmas in Hooterville
The Hillbillies spend the Christmas holiday in Hooterville, where Eb courts Elly May and Granny pursues Sam Drucker.
Edgar Buchanan..............................Uncle Joe
Mike Minor..Steve
Meredith Macrae...............................Billie Jo
Tom Lester..Eb

This rare portrait captures the casts of "The Beverly Hillbillies," "Petticoat Junction," and "Green Acres" for the Thanksgiving episode: (Left to right) Max Baer, Meredith MacRae, Eddie Albert, Lori Saunders, Irene Ryan, Frank Cady, Nancy Kulp, Linda Kaye Henning, Buddy Ebsen, Donna Douglas, Mike Minor, Eva Gabor, June Lockhart, Tom Lester, Edgar Buchanan, and Ray Bailey.

PHOTO BY GABI RONA

Linda Kaye Henning.............................Betty Jo
Lori Saunders..................................Bobbie Jo
Frank Cady..................................Sam Drucker
Percy Helton............................Homer Cratchit

213. Drysdale and Friend
Banker Drysdale is jailed for transporting Granny's
"white lightnin' " and Elly May's drunken bear in
Jethro's truck.
Percy Helton...........................Homer Cratchit
Stacy King.......................................Kathy
Frank Cady..................................Sam Drucker
Mike Ross......................................Sheriff
J. Pat O'Malley..................................Judge
Hank Patterson....................................Fred

214. Problem Bear
Banker Drysdale comes down with the flu, and "doctor"
Granny tries to treat him with her moonshine "serum."
Harriet MacGibbon.......................Mrs. Drysdale
Norma Varden....................Mrs. Van Ransonhoff

215. Jethro the Flesh Peddler
Jethro sets himself up in an office in Drysdale's bank as
a Hollywood talent agent.
Pamela Rodgers...................................Bunny
Roy Clark...................................Cousin Roy
Judy Jordan..................................Chauffeur

216. Cousin Roy in Movieland
Jethro turns down Cousin Roy as a client for his new
Hollywood talent agency.
Pamela Rodgers...................................Bunny
Roy Clark...................................Cousin Roy
Judy Jordan..................................Chauffeur

217. Jed Clampett Enterprises
Drysdale finally gets a paying tenant for the fifth floor of
his bank building—by evicting Jethro and renting it to
Jed.
Venita Wolf.......................................Suzy
Jeanette O'Connor..................................Lee
Percy Helton...........................Homer Cratchit
Judy Jordan..................................Chauffeur
Seamon Glass.....................................Julie

218. The Phantom Fifth Floor
A building inspector probes the strangely assorted Jed Clampett enterprises on the fifth floor of Drysdale's bank building.
Herb Vigran.....................................Armstrong
Seamon Glass...Julie

219. The Hired Gun
Banker Drysdale hires troubleshooter Homer Bedloe to evict the Clampetts from his building's fifth floor.
Charles Lane....................................Bedloe
Percy Helton..............................Homer Cratchit

220. The Happy Bank
A beautiful secretary at Drysdale's bank breaks the heel of her shoe and hobbles to "cobbler" Jed Clampett for a lift.
Percy Helton..............................Homer Cratchit
Judy Jordan...Babs
Ingeborg Kjeldsen....................................Carol
Georgene Barnes....................................Jeanie
Jeanette O'Connor..................................Linda
Dee Carroll............................Pregnant Woman

221. Sam Drucker's Visit
Sam Drucker of "Petticoat Junction" wins a trip to Hollywood, and Granny assumes that he's come to marry her.
Larry Pennell.............................Dash Riprock
Lori Saunders...............................Bobbie Jo
Frank Cady.................................Sam Drucker

222. The Guru
Jethro reads a book about yoga and decides to become a guru, much to Granny's disgust.
Harriet MacGibbon........................Mrs. Drysdale
Ray Kellogg.................................Policeman
William Mimms....................................Guru

223. The Jogging Clampetts
When the Clampetts take up jogging as a hobby, Mr. Drysdale puts on a jogging suit to trot along and seek new business for his bank.
Harriet MacGibbon........................Mrs. Drysdale
Paul Newlan.............................Jason Detweiler

224. Collard Greens an' Fatback
The Drysdales sell their mansion to singer Pat Boone,
who is intrigued by Granny's steaming backyard kettle
of hillbilly stew.
Pat Boone...Himself
Harriet MacGibbon........................Mrs. Drysdale

225. Back to the Hills
The Hillbillies go back to the hills to find Elly May a
husband, much to the dismay of banker Drysdale.
Rob Reiner...Mitch
B. Robert Corff...Boy
Bonnie Boland...Girl

226. The Hills of Home
The Clampetts arrive in the mountain town of Silver
Dollar City, where Granny starts a feud with an old rival,
Elverna Bradshaw.
Walter Woolf King...................................Parnell
Elvia Allman...Elverna
Lloyd Heller..Shad
Shug Fisher..Shorty
Rob Reiner...Mitch
Chick Allen..Himself

227. Silver Dollar City Fair
Granny continues her efforts to get Elly May married,
extolling the young girl's virtues to every bachelor she
meets.
Elvia Allman...Elverna
Lloyd Heller...Shad
Shug Fisher..Shorty
Chick Allen..Himself

228. Jane Finds Elly A Man
Birdwatcher Jane Hathaway hikes into the woods and
finds a man for Elly May.
Shug Fisher..Shorty
Hope Wainwright..............................Stewardess
Roger Torrey.......................................Matthew
Jerry Brutsche...................................Messenger

COURTESY OF HOWARD FRANK ARCHIVES/FILMWAYS

Elverna Bradshaw
(Elvia Allman) is infuriated
by the caricature-rendering
by her archrival, Granny.

229. Wedding Plans
The Clampetts rehearse for Elly May's wedding to backwoodsman Matthew Templeton, unaware that banker Drysdale wants it stopped.
Shug Fisher..Shorty
Elvia Allman.....................................Elverna
Roger Torrey....................................Matthew
Jerry Brutsche....................................Robert

230. Jed Buys Central Park
Elly May's wedding is called off, so Jed plans to buy Central Park and move the family to New York to find another eligible suitor.
Phil Silvers..Shifty
Shug Fisher..Shorty
Roger Torrey....................................Matthew
Pat Winters....................................Stewardess

231. The Clampetts in New York

Con man Shifty Shafer sells the Clampetts Central Park and then unloads on them three other New York landmarks.

Phil Silvers..Shifty
John Cliff......................................Policeman
Norman Grabowski............................Mugger #1
Bucklind Beery...............................Mugger #2
Dick Wesson.....................................Cabbie
Peggy Russell................................Old Woman

232. Manhattan Hillbillies

Drysdale and Jane arrive in New York to persuade the Hillbillies to abandon their half-built cabin in Central Park and return home.

Sammy Davis, Jr....................................Pat
Norman Grabowski............................Mugger #1
Bucklind Berry...............................Mugger #2
Lennie Bremen....................................Cabby
Sean McClory..................................Policeman

Sammy Davis, Jr., plays an Irish policeman in the New York City episodes.

COURTESY OF FILMWAYS

Gun-totin' Granny was ready
to shoot the pants off anybody
who wronged her—'specially the law!

COURTESY OF VIACOM

233. Home Again
Granny insists she doesn't need glasses, although she carries on a conversation with a pet seal, thinking it's Elly's new boyfriend.

Brian West . . . . Dr. Bob Graham
John Scott Lindsey . . . . Jimmy
Judy McConnell . . . . Secretary

234. Shorty Kellems Moves West
Shorty Kellems, proprietor of the hotel in Silver Dollar City, sells out and leaves the hills to join the Clampetts in California.

Harriet MacGibbon . . . . Mrs. Drysdale
Judy Jordan . . . . Miss Switzer
Shug Fisher . . . . Shorty
Judy McConnell . . . . Miss Leeds

235. Midnight Shorty
Drysdale, trying to get Shorty to deposit money in his bank, plies the visiting mountaineer with girls and games.

Shug Fisher . . . . Shorty
Danielle Mardi . . . . Miss Thompson
Judy Jordan . . . . Miss Switzer
Bettina Brenna . . . . Miss Buckles
Judy McConnell . . . . Miss Leeds
Ruth Ko . . . . Dealer

236. Shorty Go Home
Granny uses her shotgun as she punishes Jethro for leading too wild a Hollywood life with Shorty Kellems.

Shug Fisher . . . . Shorty
Danielle Mardi . . . . Miss Thompson
Judy Jordan . . . . Miss Switzer
Bettina Brenna . . . . Miss Buckles
Judy McConnell . . . . Miss Leeds

237. The Hero
Mrs. Drysdale gives her nephew, who has just left the Air Force, a hero's welcome and a job as vice president in her husband's bank.

Soupy Sales . . . . Lance Bradford
Harriet MacGibbon . . . . Mrs. Drysdale
Danielle Mardi . . . . 1st Girl
Ruth Ko . . . . 2nd Girl
Carolyn Williamson . . . . 3rd Girl
Gloria Hill . . . . 4th Girl

238. Our Hero the Banker
Mrs. Drysdale's nephew, who possesses a wealth of
confidence but no talent, takes over Drysdale's private
office at his Beverly Hills Bank.
Soupy Sales...................................Lance Bradford

239. Buzz Bodine, Boy General
The Clampetts visit Hooterville, and Jed arranges to go
into the airline business with pilot Steve Elliott.
Mike Minor.....................................Steve Elliot

240. The Clampett-Hewes Empire
Banker Drysdale eagerly prepares to set up the deal for a
new airline formed by Jed and farmer Howard Hewes,
mistaking him for famous millionaire Howard Hughes
from a phone conversation with Jed.

241. What Happened to Shorty?
Jed Clampett and Shad Heller conspire to line up Shorty
Kellems as a husband for the strong-minded widow,
Elverna Bradshaw.
Shug Fisher...................................Shorty
Lloyd Heller...................................Shad
Elvia Allman..................................Elverna

242. Marry Me, Shorty
The Hillbillies unsuccessfully conspire to get Shorty
Kellems married to Elverna Bradshaw.
Shug Fisher...................................Shorty
Lloyd Heller...................................Shad
Elvia Allman..................................Elverna

243. Shorty Spits the Hook
Elusive Shorty Kellems gets off the marital hook by
convincing his eager bride-to-be that he is an inveterate
gambler.
Shug Fisher...................................Shorty
Lloyd Heller...................................Shad
Elvia Allman..................................Elverna

244. Three-Day Reprieve
Jed and Shad Heller discover it's a full-time job keeping
Shorty Kellems corralled until his marriage to the
indomitable Elverna.
Shug Fisher...................................Shorty
Lloyd Heller...................................Shad

Not used to modern bathrooms,
the Hillbillies scrub in the tub.

COURTESY OF VIACOM

245. The Wedding
Shorty Kellems again short-circuits fiancée Elverna's
wedding plans, this time by marrying Mr. Drysdale's
prettiest secretary.
Shug Fisher...Shorty

246. Annul That Marriage

The Clampetts set up a miniature farm so Shorty's bride Gloria can sample farm life, and soon the exhausted girl is delighted to hear she's not really married.

Shug Fisher..Shorty

247. Hotel for Women

The Hillbillies leave Shorty Kellems temporarily in charge of the Clampett mansion, and he turns it into a hotel for single secretaries.

Shug Fisher..Shorty

248. Simon Legree Drysdale

The Clampett mansion is set up as a hotel for women, and banker Drysdale decides to extort a few dollars from his secretary guests.

Scene stealers: It was usually a toss-up between Granny and Jethro as to who carried the scene. Jethro is the obvious bearer here.

249. Honest John Returns
The Hillbillies again meet "Honest John," the confidence man who had sold them half of Manhattan and then returned their money.
Phil Silvers....................................Honest John

250. Honesty Is the Best Policy
Jed prepares to underwrite con man Honest John's scheme to drill a channel in the mountains to draw off Los Angeles's smog.
Phil Silvers....................................Honest John

251. The Pollution Solution
The Hillbillies plan to go to Washington to give the President their $95 million fortune to help fight air pollution.
Rich Little...Himself
Bill Beckett.......................................Milkman

252. The Clampetts in Washington
The Clampetts arrive in Washington, D.C., to give the President $95 million to help in the fight against smog.
Phil Silvers...................................Shifty Shafer
Keith Rogers.......................................Steward
Richard Erdman.......................................Guard
Kathleen Freeman.............................Flo Shafer
Al Lanti...Cab Driver

253. Jed Buys the Capitol
Shifty Shafer sells Jed the Capitol, the Pentagon, and various other choice pieces of Washington real estate.
Phil Silvers...................................Shifty Shafer
Kathleen Freeman.............................Flo Shafer

254. Mark Templeton Arrives
Romance enters Elly May's life in a big way when Navy Lt. Mark Templeton arrives at the Clampett mansion to pay a visit.
Roger Torrey.............................Mark Templeton
Sherry Miles.........................Darlene Mattingly

255. Don't Marry a Frogman
Granny, convinced that Elly May's Navy frogman boyfriend is actually half-frog, attempts to cure him.
Roger Torrey.............................Mark Templeton

COURTESY OF VIACOM

Clem the goat makes his debut performance with Granny and Elly May.

256. Doctor Cure My Frog
Granny consults a psychiatrist to give "modern medicine" a chance to keep frogman Mark Templeton from turning into a real frog.
Roger Torrey.............................Mark Templeton
Richard Deacon............................Dr. Klingner

257. Do You Elly Take This Frog
Granny takes a sleeping potion and has a nightmare that Elly May marries a giant frog.
Roger Torrey.............................Mark Templeton
Vincent Perry............................Judge Marshall
Richard Deacon............................Dr. Klingner

258. The Frog Family

Granny battles to keep her family out of the swimming pool, convinced that if they get wet they'll turn into frogs.

Roger Torrey...........................Mark Templeton
Richard Deacon...........................Dr. Klingner

259. Farm in the Ocean

Frogman Mark Templeton unsuccessfully tries to convince Granny that man's future lies on the ocean floor.

Roger Torrey...........................Mark Templeton
Richard Deacon...........................Dr. Klingner
Warrene Ott...........................Sharon Klingner

260. Shorty to the Rescue

Granny sends back home to the hills for Shorty Kellems to help break up Elly May's romance with Mark Templeton.

Roger Torrey...........................Mark Templeton
Richard Deacon...........................Dr. Klingner
Shug Fisher.......................................Shorty

Granny and Elly May watch out for Indians when they think they are victims of a warpath.

COURTESY OF VIACOM

261. Welcome to the Family
Granny thinks Shorty Kellems has turned into a seal because he ignored her warnings about swimming in the Clampett pool.
Roger Torrey..............................Mark Templeton
Lori Saunders...............................Betty Gordon
Shug Fisher...Shorty

262. The Great Revelation
Granny is finally convinced that Elly May's boyfriend, Mark Templeton, is a human being—not half-frog, as she suspected.
Roger Torrey..............................Mark Templeton
Danielle Mardi...........................Helen Thompson

263. The Grunion Invasion
Jed, Granny, Elly May, and Jethro man the battlements against an expected invasion of grunion, which they believe to be hostile aliens.
Danielle Mardi...........................Helen Thompson
Jerry Brutsche..................................Surfer #1
Sue Bernard....................................Surfer #2

264. The Girls from Grun
The Hillbillies, encouraged by Mr. Drysdale, continue to guard the Malibu beach and repel the mythical grunion invaders.
Danielle Mardi...........................Helen Thompson
David Moses..Medic
Sue Bernard...Girl
Jane Axell.....................................Secretary #1

265. The Grun Incident
Drysdale's downtrodden bank secretaries organize to fight for better wages and working conditions.
Danielle Mardi...........................Helen Thompson
Jane Axell..Ulla
Foster Brooks..Man
Francisco Ortega...................................Guard
Momo Yashima......................................Girl #1
Roberta Carol......................................Girl #2

266. Women's Lib

Granny and Elly May join the Women's Liberation Movement and leave all household chores to Jed and Jethro with disastrous results.

Danielle Mardi......................................Helen
Momo Yashima......................................Susie
Fuji..Banzai
Francisco Ortega...................................Guard

267. The Teahouse of Jed Clampett

The Hillbilly womenfolk leave the Clampett mansion, but Jed and Jethro replace them with a trio of Japanese beauties.

Charles Lane...........................Foster Phinney
Lori Saunders..................................Betty
Danielle Mardi.................................Helen
Fuji..Banzai

(The character Foster Phinney was named after the show's assistant director, Foster Phinney.)

Jethro soups up the old truck fer somethin' more akin to his playboy image.

COURTESY OF VIACOM

268. The Palace of Clampett San
Jed and Jethro enjoy an idyllic interval of living like
Oriental potentates, waited on hand and foot by three
lovely Japanese women.
Charles Lane.............................Foster Phinney
Miko Mayama................................Miko
Momo Yashima................................Susie
Lori Saunders................................Betty
Danielle Mardi...............................Helen
Sumi Haru................................Girl #1
Kazuka Sakura.............................Girl #2

269. Lib and Let Lib
Granny and Elly, assured of their equal rights, return to
the Clampett mansion.
Danielle Mardi.............................Helen
Miko Mayama...............................Miko
Fuji...Banzai

270. Elly, the Working Girl
Elly May gets a job at Mr. Drysdale's Commerce Bank
and moves into Jane Hathaway's apartment.
Danielle Mardi.............................Helen
Charles Lane...........................Foster Phinney

271. Elly, the Secretary
Jethro leaves home when he learns his ugly childhood
sweetheart is coming for a visit, not knowing she has
become a beauty contest winner.
Louellen Aden............................Louellen Aden

272. Love Finds Jane Hathaway
Dick Bremerkamp, a penniless actor, learns the
Clampetts are millionaires and uses Miss Jane to get to
Elly May.
Mike Minor............................Bremerkamp
Charles Lane...........................Foster Phinney

273. The Clampetts Meet Robert Audubon Getty
A fortune-hunting young man decides to marry into the
Hillbilly family.
Mike Minor............................Bremerkamp
Charles Lane.............................Phinney

274. Jethro Returns
Jane Hathaway learns her new boyfriend is a fortune
hunter who would like to marry Elly May and her
family's millions.
Mike Minor............................Bremerkamp

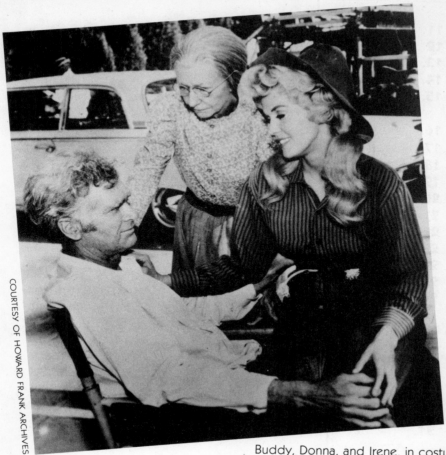

COURTESY OF HOWARD FRANK ARCHIVES

Buddy, Donna, and Irene, in costume
but out of character, share a joke on the set.

ANSWERS TO TRIVIA QUESTIONS

1. Daisy May Moses.
2. Elly May. Occupation: movie star. Real Name: Homer Noodleman. (Actor Larry Pennell played the role.)
3. Mr. Martin Van Ransohoff. Jim Backus, who played Mr. Howell
   on Gilligan's Island, played Ransohoff.
4. Napoleon, Tennessee.
5. O.K. Oil Company of Tulsa, Oklahoma.
6. A new kind of money called "Million dollars."
7. The Clampetts resided at 518 Crestview Drive, Beverly Hills,
   California.
8. Amos Hogg.
9. Hoot Gibson.
10. The Happy Gizzard.

11. Bug Tussle Biltmore.
12. Mother Myrtle's Magic Mixture.
13. Doctor Daisy's Death Defier.
14. Usually a $20 bill—waved under his nose.
15. Top three: "Red-neck Romance," "Turkey in the Straw," and "There's a Hog Jowl Where Your Heart Ought to Be."
16. The Boston Strong Girl.
17. His real first name was Adonis.
18. Henry Gibson.
19. Fifty cents a week.
20. Bill Baldwin.
21. Thirty-two rooms and fourteen baths.
22. Rose Ellen Moses.
23. Nancy.
24. Elly May Margaret Clampett.
25. Famous Ozark fisherman, Jim Owen.
26. A muscle spasm peculiar to bankers. Drysdale suffered from this when clenching money; his fist would lock up. Jane Hathaway had to cure him by striking a particular part of his neck with a karate chop.
27. Jerry Scoggins.
28. Joe Depew.
29. Big Jethro.
30. Winston.
31. "The Beverly Hillbillies," "Petticoat Junction," and "Green Acres."
32. Jethro.
33. He whittled a wooden statue of Granny holding a jar of preserves. (The statue was actually carved by Peter Engler of Silver Dollar City in the Ozarks, who had been commissioned by Paul Henning.)
34. "Ain't She Sweet" ("From her head down to her feet").
35. A derby; a big, orange flower pattern.
36. The name of the English butler who lived in their castle. The Hillbillies misunderstood his name to be a salutation (such as Aloha) and spouted "Faversham" when meaning hello or goodbye.
37. To hide the scar from when he once asked his father: "Dad, there must be something in this world more important than money?"
38. She applied a poultice; one time she even considered a "head transplant" for Mr. Drysdale.
39. Canada.
40. Yodeling, playin' the pie-annie (piano).

AFTERWORD

On the Silver Anniversary of this show's first season there is a resurgence of Hillbillymania again in the country. The show has gone unrecognized for so long that a renaissance is due. The elements of this comeback are evident. The sophisticated viewers who originally pulled their shades down to enjoy the show might possibly realize that the show was not so bad afterall. It contained no vulgar humor. It centered around a good, down-to-earth family. Its humor was simple. Like a fine chocolate that's easily unwrapped and melted in the mouth, the Hillbillies were easily enjoyed. They were the hassock for America's tired feet. They were easy to watch, a comfort, and pleasurable every time.

Folks have welcomed it into their homes like an old friend countless times. They still do.

The rights to syndication of the Hillbillies were sold to Viacom International, which also distributes "The Honeymooners," "The Andy Griffith Show," "I Love Lucy," "The Dick Van Dyke Show," and "All in the Family," among others. The company has only praise for the series: "By far it is our most popular and widely syndicated offering," says Viacom publicist Betsy Vorce. "It's in countless markets around the world. Fans love it and it seems to still hold up."

The show, whose perfectly cast performers are still working, can be seen in just about every major city and also on cable television. Although the cast no longer receives residuals, they still receive recognition, which pleases them.

203

"People still recognize me," says Nancy Kulp. "I can't go to the market without getting stopped by someone. I went to a dog show the other day and fans approached me for autographs. I love it."

Buddy Ebsen has requests for autographs and many times signs the photos of Jed with a "Well Doggies" or something personalized. He still catches the show occasionally. "I'll go into towns, and I'll be up at odd hours, and I sit and watch myself doing things I don't remember," Ebsen says. "And laughing."

Life goes on and so do reruns.

Actress Donna Douglas, who during the heyday of the program received the most fan mail, still loves to talk with fans who come from miles around to meet her at a personal appearance or autograph signing. The attention has not waned, and as Douglas sees it, "If the fans want to invest the time, then I'm willing."

Douglas, who has made annual paid appearances at the Ozark Extravaganza in Rolla, Missouri, every September, greets fans with a Southern "howdy," ready to sign photos. There she also visits the Memoryville U.S.A. museum that shines a special display on the show, which includes personal memorabilia from the cast and Hillbilly merchandising items.

It has been said that the sincerest form of flattery is imitation. In that case, the Hillbillies' theme song has been flattered for an array of topics. Although parodies are illegal unless authorized, the song has enjoyed much success with hundreds of radio station promotions, hucksters, and comedians alike. This, more than any other theme, has been rearranged so many times because of its instant recognition, adaptability to topics, and comedy content.

The theme was put to use, with consent of its lyricist Paul Henning, for a parody on NBC's late night hit, "Saturday Night Live," in the mid 1970s. The sketch titled "The Bel-Arabs" aired at the height of the U.S. oil crisis and starred the cast originals, Gilda Radner, Laraine Newman, John Belushi, and Dan Aykroyd.

Part of the rather tasteless theme song went like this:

> Come an' listen to m' story 'bout Sheik Ahmed
> Poor Bedouin barely kep' his family fed
> An' then one day he was shootin' at some Jews
> An' up thru the ground come bubblin ooze
>
> Oil that is . . . black gold, Texas tea. . . .
> First thing y'know, Ahmed's a billionaire,
> Kinfolk said Ahmed, move away from there
> Said Californy is th' place y' oughta be,
> So he loaded up th' jet and flew to Beverly.
>
> Hills that is . . . swimmin' pool, movie stars . . . Jews!"

The parody, expertly done by the improvisational masters of the original cast of "Saturday Night Live," was a screaming success. The skit had Aykroyd and Belushi as FBI agents coming to question the Clampetts about their fortune. Laraine Newman played Elly May and Gilda Radner portrayed a fantastic, wild Granny. The whole family spoke Arabic, which added to the humor. The show recreated the opening sequence with the Clampetts riding down a Beverly Hills street in the truck and even recreated the entrance hallway of their mansion with impeccable accuracy.

Another travesty of "The Ballad of Jed Clampett" was 1987's "Ballad of Jim & Tammy" which circulated billboards, frequented photocopy machines, and popped into mailboxes all around the country. This was in response to the Bakker/PTL scandal which received hordes of publicity.

The theme goes like this:

> Come an' listen to m' story 'bout a man named Jim.
> Poor missionary, couldn't stay away from sin.
> An' then one day Tammy was shootin' down some ludes,
> An' up from the bed come Jessica nude.
>
> Sex that is . . . blackmail, guilty pleas!
>
> Well th' first thing y' know, ol' Jim's a millionaire
> Falwell says, "Jim, move away from there."
> He said Californy is th' place y' oughta be
> So they loaded up the limo and cruised to Beverly.
>
> Pills that is . . . sex tools, gay bars!
>
> Well now it's time to say goodbye to Jim and all his kin,
> They're mighty glad you folks keep sendin' money in
> You're all invited back next week to this locality
> To watch Jerry Falwell take away their keys.
>
> Take your clothes off! Set a spell! Y'all come back now,
> y' hear?"

In the mid-1980s, a rock band calling itself "Dash Riprock" emerged and played to limited audiences around the United States. The name fit their style and people naturally associated the show with their title.

Possibly the sincerest flattery will come later in 1988 or early 1989 when a movie version of the Beverly Hillbillies will be released, according to producer David Permut. Permut, who worked on *Dragnet*, the motion picture parody starring Dan

Aykroyd and Tom Hanks in 1987, expects this one to fare just as well, if not better.

"I think the Beverly Hillbillies idea works," Permut says. "The fish out of water concept is great." He plans to script the movie using the same characters and story line, basically. The roles will be recast, but a possible cameo by the originals has been discussed.

Dan Aykroyd as Jed? Maybe.

ABOUT THE AUTHOR

Stephen Cox received his bachelor's degree in journalism and communication arts from Park College in Kansas City, Missouri. He has written freelance for *Comedy Magazine* and collaborated on six books about his favorite comedy team, The Three Stooges. Cox was named Journalist of the Year for 1987 by the Missouri College Newspaper Association. He makes his home in St. Louis.